ISBN 978-1-330-75193-0
PIBN 10100734

FB &c Ltd, Dalton House, 60 Windsor Avenue, London, SW19 2RR.
Company number 08720141. Registered in England and Wales.

For support please visit www.forgottenbooks.com

THE
POEMS OF ṬUKĀRĀMA

TRANSLATED AND RE-ARRANGED, WITH NOTES AND AN INTRODUCTION, BY J. NELSON FRASER, M.A., INDIAN EDUCATION DEPARTMENT, AND K. B. MARATHI, B.A., LL.B., LATE OF THE BOMBAY JUDICIAL SERVICE

VOLUME III

THE CHRISTIAN LITERATURE SOCIETY FOR INDIA

LONDON MADRAS CALCUTTA RANGOON COLOMBO

1915

PREFACE

THE appearance of this third volume, like that of the second, is due to the liberality of the Bombay Government, who have contributed half the cost of its production. And once more we offer our thanks to the Christian Literature Society.

The principles on which the translation has been made remain the same. In this volume, however, many abhangas on familiar themes have been omitted, and many easy lines from other abhangas.

The index is continued. We regret to find that though there are many editions of Tukā, there is not one which follows the numbering of the *Indo-Prakash* edition, which is, however, much the best. It is now out of print. Our index is therefore not of much use—but this is only a specimen of the inconveniences which beset any attempt to deal with *orientalia*.

In the preface to our second volume we appealed to the public to bring to our notice any written or published accounts of Tukā or critical examinations of his work. We know that many such exist, but in the disorganized state of the literary world of India, it is difficult to find them. We venture, therefore, to repeat our appeal, as we still hope, in a concluding volume, to deal with the life of Tukā and the history of Pandharpur.

J. NELSON FRASER.

July 5, 1915.

CONTENTS

Autobiography

I.—Thoughts about the World

2649

THOUGH I have abandoned the world, yet desires arise in my heart; what am I to do? Let me cast at thy feet this bundle of my body. As to whether we do or do not, rules and prohibitions may guide us; but if we cannot discern their inner spirit, we shall waste our labour. Tukā says, Give me not life on the surface, but hide thyself within me.

2650

THROUGH sin, truth has been utterly destroyed. The clouds shrink from falling down, the crops have forsaken the soil. Tukā says, The Vedas have lost all strength and courage.

2651

SO unfordable is the stream of life that we know not how to cross it. The savage beasts of lust and wrath fill us with dread. The eddies of illusion and desire whirl formidably round us. The billows of desire surge up; worldly transactions toss men to and fro. As the only means of passage, Tukā seats himself in the boat of the name.

2652

WHEN it is well with you, all accompany you; when it is ill, no one stays till the end. Neither father, mother, nor mistress stays—why need I mention others? Tukā says, Mankind are doublefaced, they prey upon you when they see their chance.

11.—Humility, Sin and Misery

2653

I CALL myself thy slave, yet I do thee no service. I fill my belly like an insolent knave. Yet how can falsehood prevail at thy feet! Thou knowest the heart, O God! We ourselves know that we have behaved falsely; to say anything else would be untrue. Tukā says, So guilty am I; thus let me be known to thee.

2654

I AM pained by what has happened to-day; the world has greatly troubled me. I know not when thou wilt break this tie; I sit remembering thy feet. The thoughts of others bar our path, their pain and pleasure, good and evil. Tukā says, It is best to live by oneself, then we put an end to all ties.

2655

MY conduct in lives past was not pure, hence I lost thy feet. But when I look to this present life, it seems that my store of merit has borne fruit. Now, O Lord of Pandhari, show me mercy. I am wicked and full of evil deeds; I am grievously tormented by the world. I am so troubled by wrath and desire that I cannot reach thee, O God! Neither this place nor that is open to me. I run after thy name, O come speedily to me, says Tukā.

2656

IN early days, I had never heard of this step; otherwise, should I have made any mistake about it? Why should I plunge myself in falsehood? Why should I put a needless burden on my head? Tukā says, Why should I enter the womb again now? Why should I make myself a slave of my family?

2657

I AM so vile that I feel neither love nor affection; nay, if I am honoured, I am all the more provoked by this. Curse my ungrateful body! It feels no obligation for kindness done to it. It takes no pleasure even in costly dishes of sweet food. I can see in me no good qualities of my own; who can say what the store of my past is like? Tukā says, I know not what Pānduranga has seen in me that he keeps me at his feet.

2658

THOU shalt be sung by the lips of unnumbered men, for thou hast unnumbered servants. Then what account shall be made of me? I am fit for nothing but contempt. Thou art always prosperous. O Nārāyana endued with skill! Tukā says, Such are the spirits of the Kali age; none will pity these sinful wretches.

2659

I HAVE no use for thee now, O Shame! get hence, let me remember Rāma. Through yielding to thee I ruined myself; I made myself the slave of this evil world. You made my mother's house strange to me; you decked yourself out and actually led me astray. To gain pleasure I carried a wife on my shoulder; she brought a host of children upon me. I was taken before the four judges and the five; I was not suffered to entertain pure aspirations. Tukā says, Now I will drag thee across thorns; I have made God my champion.

2660

IN the hour of my birth why was there a good omen seen? Now you withdraw and hide yourself. I never asked for this gift of speech, a thing dry, fruitless and external. What is mere prolixity apart from truth? Speech should be such as to attain its purpose; all else is chaff. Tukā says, Who is it you are tormenting in this way? You do not consider this, O Pānduranga!

2661

WHEREVER I go, I am a vendor of stale goods; I can see no prospect of gain. Were the lines drawn upon my forehead propitious, should I suffer this toil and care? Thou wilt not receive me as thy own; and the worldly comforts I once had I have lost. My allotted portion has now once been given me to endure. Time is stealing from me my capital, life. When did I hear of thy fame? How is it I lose my life? says Tukā.

2662

THAT thou shouldest accept me, O God, no such thought enters my mind. There is a stain now on both of us, bringing shame on the relation of worshippers and worshipped. Even in solitude my mind is restless; it will not stay still a moment. My legs are fettered by dignity thrust on me; my friends have put a rope on my neck. Now that my body has caught sight of these pleasures it has grown addicted to them; my mouth does not relish stale food. Tukā says, I have become a pit full of vices; indolence and laziness have grown upon me.

2663

MY idle talk is looked on as poetry, but it is not moist with moisture from my innermost being. Nārāyana returns no answer to me; I have no influence over him. Why did this shameless voice utter words? I am not at heart a reflective man. Tukā says, My exertions have borne no fruit; what happened to me, O dweller in Pandhari?

2664

I HAVE power to control time; such is the boast I make; then lo! I am found lower than the lowest wretches, far away from God and blackened in the face. Once I trusted in God; I was his slave. Tukā says, I went about to raise my own dignity and importance.

2665

I PLOD along like an ass, with a burden on my back. I go where the saints wish to take me; my body is in their power. I am like a water-bag strengthened with battens of wood; within me is the strength of the food left by the saints. I never quit the highway, I never shirk my load. By the authority they possess they keep me moving; I have no cares of my own. Tukā prays earnestly, Give me no household affairs to transact.

2666

MY mind is penetrated by the thought of renouncing the world; I would fain retire to the forest. Why dost thou not bestow peace on this mind of mine? It is grieved by separation from thee. No one comes to bring me a message from Pandhari; he sends me not even a wreath from his neck. Tukā says, I abhor my life; though I serve thee, I feel ashamed while I do so.

2667

I UNDERSTAND now what my faith is like; I have harassed my soul in vain. I have strong together words and babbled on; and as the end of it all, I have gained nothing. Tukā says, I have lost both worlds; I have gained neither this world nor thy feet.

2668

I HAVE passed through many misfortunes in the world; though I have thrown them off, still there is a settled weariness in my mind. Now let me hide myself at thy feet, O God; look not for service or devotion from me. If I hear a cry that even one trouble is coming, I am full of dread; but crowds of troubles have returned on me. Tuka says, My measure is heaped up; separation from thee causes me great agony.

2669

YOU never visited me even in a dream, I am left dejected; how is it possible I could ever have seen him talking to me?

2670

SLOTH has laid hold of me—Run, Run,. O Pānduranga! Bodily sensations pass over me; vice showers its blows upon me. Let Nārāyana approach and banish my evil habits. Though I was near, I have drifted far away; O God! take me by the hand. This is why I entreat thee time after time. Tukā says, O Pānduranga, do not keep me far from thee!

2671

THOUGH I possess myself of all wisdom, yet, O Nārāyana, I do not reach thee. Though men honour me, I do not reach thy feet. Though I make myself indifferent to the world, still thy secret is far from me. Though I put forth strenuous efforts, I must call myself thy slave and worshipper. Tukā says, Unless thou show thy secret thyself, who can learn it?

2672

WE have no firm devotion to thee; how then can we blame thee? We ask wages for service never rendered. We have not worshipped thee, our faith is not pure; but the blame lies on our destiny. Unnumbered worshippers there have been who renounced the world and subdued their lusts. No such vigour have I shown, yet I wish to meet thee. Of thy compassion fulfil this desire; vindicate thy name! Tukā says, Though a child be an idiot, yet his father and mother do carefully maintain him.

III.—Prayers

2673

IF I merely send thee a message how can it reach thy feet? Hence I have surrendered my very life to thee. Tukā says, Give me salvation into my own hands; this is what I importune thee for.

2674

I DESIRED in my heart to be one of the foremost; yet I hung back through shame. I call joyfully upon thee, yet even so thou hidest thyself. Give me my own—what I compassed by devoted faith. O Stay of the world, says Tukā, gratify thy self-willed child!

2675

FOR once set me free from woe, by opening the net of sin. Long, long, hast thou kept me suffering; now, O Pānduranga, set me free! Tukā says, I will make an offering of my body; I will wave my head round thee like a lamp and throw it away.

2676

SAVE me from self-conceit by making me wretched, so that my life in the world may be wasted.

2677

SUPPORTED by the testimony of my own mind I relate what has happened to me, in the story of all my life. It is for you, in virtue of your power, to take kindly care of us; if you hold us aloof, how can we live? Why else was it that I left the word of 'I' and 'mine,' O generous one! Tukā says, Without your help we are left to destiny in the world.

2678

AN unprotected stranger, wretched, lowly and artless, I roll helpless in thy temple-court. Cast thy glance upon me, as the tortoise looks on its young; make me to apprehend what knowledge of God means. Tukā says, I fall at thy feet,—body, speech, and spirit; I have none besides thee.

IV.—How He Awoke

2679

WHAT we need in this world is a father who can secure liberation for his progeny, but thou, O Dnyānadeva, didst put away the sins of thy father and mother. My own father was likewise learned, hence I began to meditate on God. Tukā says, I am my father's legitimate child; fulfil my craving for knowledge of Brahmā.

2680

I WAS tormented by 'mine' and 'thine'; I did not see what was close to me. The abode that I was seeking I possess; my desire is satisfied. My only fear, savs Tukā, is lest Viṭṭhobā should be angry with me.

2681

NOTHING of the world clung to me; I became solitary; I knew no other attachment. See how the cowherd tortured me and drove me mad! He attached me to himself and hid me in him. Tukā says, I did not comprehend this till I was ruined by devotion to him.

2682

I WAS well off till I met him; then this thief stripped me. He swept away everything, and left me an empty ruined house. My mind, the source of contemplation, my only wealth, he has carried off; Tukā says, He has made me what I was to begin with.

2683

ONCE I debated with myself how to keep myself alive in this world. Then came the Dweller in the heart to my aid, and revealed to me that there is no such thing as destruction. I was plunged in a sea of gloom, wondering how to reach the shore. Tukā says, My life was full of misery, my soul was troubled.

2684

WHO would touch things once offered to God? That would wrest them from their purpose. Once for all this body has been offered to him, so anything that happens to it will be welcome. A load I carried once, but the bitterness of it has been put far from me; my body is now but an empty storehouse. Tukā says, Desire made me suffer misery, so I have banished the accursed thing.

2685

I WAS caught by the press-gang as I stepped forward to meet the world, but on the way I met Viṭṭhobā and he took compassion on me. I had a heavy load on my head, says Tukā; I was anxiously saying to myself, What generous man will meet me?

2686

WE are alone in a strange land, we have missed the road and lost all our bearings; now should any one take us by the hand and lead us home, what return can we make for his kindness? Even so I stood stark naked, O Keshiraja, I felt ashamed I could do thee no service. I was like a child whose mother cast him forth with a great throe, heedless even if the spot were fit for his birth; when heat and thirst and hunger set him screaming, she would put him to her breast—what shall I say of it? I was like a great criminal that goes forth to die, with an iron pole on his shoulder. Yet, says Tukā, this is what happened: Some one snatched me away and set me in shelter behind him.

2687

I LEFT the world on my own impulse; I was indeed heartily sick of it. Two things that are different cannot be forced to combine, just as buttermilk is for ever separate from butter. Both are produced by churning one substance, and different names are given to them. Chaff and grain are distinguished from each other by their properties. Tukā says, Where could a pearl ever find a dwelling place, if the mother-of-pearl were crushed?

2688

WHEN I consider, I find it was a good thing; so much I have learned. I made a clean sweep of all that I once cared for, because I perceived the great distinction. My body seems to be at rest, likewise my thoughts and feelings. Tukā says, Very fortunately God chose me and picked me up.

2689

THIS was the original step that averted my pangs; I presented my body at your feet; I was set free from toil and redeemed. Now I shall not suffer my own authority to guide me. Tukā stands apart from the world, far from all its worries.

2690

I PRACTISED neither meditation nor penance, I used no violence to my mind, I laid no restraints on it. Standing where I was I cried to thee, to rescue me in my strait. I brought and offered thee no water; by meditation alone I served thee; what I spent was spent alone. Says Tukā, My generous master accepted it in all sincerity.

2691

MY mother grew weary of carrying me in the womb, so she delivered me; but she took no care that the spot was undefiled. She suffered agonies of heat and thirst and hunger,—why should she put me to her breast? The stake was on my own shoulders, I was on the road to death, yet even then I committed grievous crimes. Then, says Tukā, this was what happened to me: He touched me with his hand and set me behind his back.

2692

LOVE for home and mankind drove me mad; how can I tell this to thee? My face was blackened with shame; I changed my own mind; I was not ashamed of myself, O Pānduranga! How can I bring these complaints before thee? What will your life or mine be like afterwards? For whose sake now should I live in the world? I have wound up my own affairs myself. Tukā says, I have broken through the customs of my family; I wait in patience at thy feet.

2693

SHOULD a jewel fall into the jaws of an alligator, a man of courage can pluck it forth with his hand; but the mind of a fool cannot be persuaded to the right path. The milk of a tortoise may feed an army. If you wander over the whole world you may perhaps find a hare with horns. If you rub sand very carefully you may perhaps extract divine oil from it. A hooded cobra provoked to fury you may perhaps hold in your hand like a flower. Lo! By the joy of Brahmā, Tukā the greatest of sinners was saved.

V.—His own disqualifications

2694

WHY hast thou so exalted me, O Pānduranga? What business was it of mine to do all this talking, to proclaim God's praises or feast

Brāmhanas? Nobody sees that I am merely an instrument, says Tukā.

2695

As you have accepted me, carry my burden; let no idea come between us. I am a slow-witted creature, how can I furnish faith enough? Accept in all sincerity such service as I can offer. Tukā says, I implore your mercy, for I am a slow-witted creature.

2696

ALL I can do is to upbraid the world; this is the portion allotted me. I gather the fruit ordained for me; my fate is decided The thoughts of other men do not harmonize with my mind. Tukā is all forlorn; women and children revile him.

2697

I AM not bold in assemblies, to stand up and speak out before men. I have led a solitary life, I have seen no companion to speak to. Now, O Nārāyana, you know all that has passed between us; see, it will move you with compassion. My intellect fails in consistency; I have not kept myself fully conscious though I tried to. In what life shall I receive strength? When will there be a decision concerning me? These now are my last words in all truth. You must protect, says Tukā, him who has come to you for protection.

2698

SHOULD destiny send the Ganges to an idle man, ought people to refuse to bathe in it? Should the wishing-cow stand in a Manga's yard, ought Brāmhanas not to bow to her? Should a leprous man take the magic-stone and make gold with it, ought we to refuse it as impure? Should a village officer be a man of low caste, ought we to refuse to obey him? Tukā likewise is sealed to be an officer of faith with Viṭṭhobā; if men heed him not their faces shall be blackened.

VI.—His Motives and the Nature of his Mission

2700

THIS speech of mine, which is a gift of thine, delivers answers; they are not pieced together from the diverse opinions of men. Tukā says, Pānduranga has raised a shelter over my head; he has increased this juice within my frame.

2701

IT is I who feel myself speaking, but it is God who makes me speak. Dull and vulgar souls, however, do not comprehend this. It is a thing unheard of, a gift of God's favour. Tukā says, This is why I go about proclaiming it.

2702

THIS secret, though I proclaim it, is not comprehended; this gives rise to errors. Whoso first keeps his mind under control, he first will pass under the authority I have assumed. If a man is not hungry, he will not welcome food, he will find no flavour in it; even so an obstinate man will find reason distasteful. Tukā says, We must watch ourselves; we cannot at present restrain other people.

2703

I HAVE laid open this treasure-house with a just measure in my hand. We have raised a loud uproar of Hari's name; let all the past vanish. There is a plenteous harvest in the land; the bad season is over. Let all take their fill, says Tukā, great and small alike.

2704

IN the market-place I unfastened my bundle, I set out my grain for sale. I gave all the authorities their dues, I finished with all troublesome requisitions. I sat there with a true measure in my hand, a measure respected by the four castes. My customers, the saints, came there enquiring for good stuff. I have shaken the grain out of my *dhotur*, I have paid off the market dues early in the morning, everything was peacefully concluded. Hurry up if you mean to come, such of you as are people of ours. There are three sorts of goods—best, middling and worst; there are also many differences between men, and they bring different samples. Some made a profit, others a loss; while others just realized their capital, some were bankrupt. Some sold only half their goods—few were these, yet too many. They all came together in company from the same village, but they will not depart together. Some were smugglers who avoided the authorities: they caught them and disgraced them. Some had to mortgage a share of their property, by acknowledging debts for posterity to pay off. Tukā says, We must delay no more; we must finish the stage before us.

2705

'SOMETHING for me, something for me!'—there is no use talking like this now. 'Tell us the price, tell us the price!'—let him ask the question who means to buy. Otherwise, how could any bargain be struck? There would be nothing but idle talking between me and you. If I am to profit, I must get my capital back again. Tukā says, I shall store my capital at home, so that in time of need men will apply to me.

2706

THE treasure belongs to God; I am merely appointed to receive and disburse. My own hands and feet are untainted; I know not how much there was in it before I came. God has taken my cares on himself; it is he who accomplishes everything. Tukā says, The master has the responsibility of supplying everything.

2707

WE have brought forth the essences by churning, we have separated all conditions and limitations. Tukā says, We have conferred this treasure on the world; it is not possible for us to have too much of it.

2708

WHEN any one steals up behind, he drives him far away; he turns him out of his own house and home. He crouches at your feet, and runs away if you say '*Cho!*' to him. If he smells a stranger he rises up and shakes himself; Tukā says, He puts fear into people, he does not allow anybody to share the buttermilk of his house.

2709

I AM led by the chain of love about my neck; I bark when I see it is time to bark. I am your dog, O Keshiraja, I am kept for this duty. I know who comes and goes along the high road or the bypaths. Tukā says, I keep at a distance strangers who approach, that they come not near.

2710

DOGS feel it their duty to keep watch over their own place; they will not let even the wind from a stranger approach their own house. They tear such to pieces, and rend their body. Tukā trusts nobody but God.

2711

GOD is fond of dogs, but he requires from them no service—save their presence. If you teach us, we will sit down near you, just where we are. We shall not let another dog open his mouth or bark. If you fondle a dog, says Tukā, then your association with it gives it a claim on you.

2712

BEING weary of stale food your dog makes bold to tug at your feet; Kānhobā understands that sign and gives him some warm food. We should eat whatever is set on our own dish, and by our devotion preserve our Master's love for us. Tukā says, I am an old dog; the illusion of the world has departed from me.

2713

WE will speak now even where we ought to be silent, in words for all mankind to hear at once. The shower considers not the place where it falls; men shall profit according to their faith. Tukā says, We do not care to make men contented, for that would injure both ourselves and those who come after us.

2714

WE shall bestow advice on men so far as they have a right to it; we ought to place a burden on the back of one who can bear it. Should we entrust an elephant's burden to an ant, what would come of it? Tukā says, A hunter takes with him nets, snares and axes; he uses each at the right time.

2715

WE are not like physicians, hungry after money, ready to give any one any sort of herb. We will not ruin our patients by unwholesome diet; what would be the use of friendliness or deference that led to this? Tukā says, We will scorch and burn and bleed them, for that will give them relief afterwards.

2716

SOME one may call this language of mine censure, but in truth he would be mistaken. When a man is taking a wrong path, to lead him to the right one—this both religion and morality enjoin. If he will not listen quietly, then let him be chastised; there is no sin, but merit, in this. Thereby would birth and death and sorrow be avoided; let us diminish the high importance we have given to these things. Tukā says, Unless you administer *neem* leaves, how can you heal a man of disease?

2717

SHALL I close the door or shall I guard the entrance, and how long? Whatever your commands may be, with bowed head I will carry them. Otherwise, I will speak as I see occasion, or else I will observe silence. Am I to keep awake, says Tukā, or to prevent any one from approaching?

2718

THE wealth in our house consists of jewels of words; we have swords of words to fight our way with. Words are the soul of our soul by words we will scatter wealth among mankind. Tukā says, Words are our God, we shall glorify words with worship.

2719

OF late I have been singing thy name in songs, and people honour me therefore. I take no thought for food or raiment; I have escaped the grievous oppression of the body. I am freed from all vexations concerning friends or relatives. Tukā says, Do with me now as thou wilt.

2720

IT is a sign of God's presence that when he enters a man's house, his manhood is crushed by a stone. God brings ruin with him; he suffers none to remain separate from himself. God does not leave us entangled in desire; he does not let the snare of affection touch us. God does not leave our speech entangled, or let the taint of falsehood pollute us. God rends the net of illusion, he annihilates the world. Lo! all these signs of his presence are with Tukā; God has seized this place for his own.

2721

MY mind is turned poet; God's praises flow through my mouth like a cataract. There is a road marked out before me; my own nature leads me to follow it. I sing God's excellent deeds, a theme ever new and ready to hand; I shape it as I please. I stand forward in the sight of all; I lead an army of bards that follow me. I speak out when he commands me, rendering willing service. There rains down on me a flood of satisfying gifts from his hand that stills all fear. Tukā's lord adorns him with words that he himself inspires.

2722

I SHUT the doors, or sometimes I guard the approach. Whatever orders are given me, I place them on my head; I carry out all commands. I give men the best advice I can, or sometimes I keep quiet to myself. Tukā says, I sometimes keep awake, sometimes I will not let others stir.

2723

YOU impressed upon me that it is easy to preach you; if I preserve the character of my discourse what else is necessary? Do not fail to support the system you have established; will you turn your generous self into a feeble wretch? If a man's resolution is really fixed, how can he depart from it? If a man does so he is called no more valiant, but feeble. Tukā says, What fault can you find with me now? I will purge away that fault with one word.

2724

THE story of Hari is told, a mood is inspired. Pānduranga has come to bring about the right. He gives to each what is right, he distributes his love; take it from him now to your heart's content. With this gift of his love he has comforted all; those who once sickened at it now delight in it. This poor wretch Tukā was seen by the saints; they have put him forward at their head.

2725

TO sanctify mankind is no painful toil to us; it is our delight. Tukā says, We eat great lumps of joy; you need not envy us, you too may eat.

2726

WHEN we praise a chaste wife, the unchaste feels a pang in her head. What I have said is spontaneous; I have never consulted any one about my words. When there is a fault in a man himself, it brings him a crack on his own pate; he sees sparks before his eyes. Tukā says, What can I do with such a one? I am sure to touch him on the ulcerous spot.

2727

THE man who has carnal intercourse with a slave, his ancestors are at the gate of hell—when I preach to the world in this style, nobody likes to hear it. Consider well—who is your friend in the end? Tukā says, You wretch, your end will be hell.

2728

I HAVE opened a shop to deal in the name of Rāma; I have samples of various kinds, help yourselves. O! be not slothful to buy this; I distribute it gratis. Each receives a share according to his store of merit; if you ask for too much, you will not get it. Tukā says, I have stored up the whole of this commodity, when enquiry was made concerning room for the rest of it.

2729

I AM eager to teach you, for time will soon advance and break your heads. What answer will you give him then? Now, though you have found God, you stay aloof from him. Your outward pretences in this world are like a juggler's disguises; but every gewgaw will fall off you. Tukā says, Why have you taken such care of refuse?

2730

IF you undertake a thing, what is impossible? In a moment you can turn a mountain into a mustard-seed. I cannot endure the blows of men; it is obvious; you can see it; they destroy my life. Lightly in jest, I first began to speak; do not remember this! Make me ignorant and humble, more so than I am, O Infinite One! Make me able to enjoy thee, says Tukā; I care nought for men.

2731

MY poems are not minted coins, yet good people accept them. They are indeed a spring welling up with butter; it will do you good to eat it. Tukā says, God drove me violently forward; a great inspiration came upon me.

2732

THE secret aim of all jackals is eggs; when they have got hold of them they load up their mouths. O you donkeys! Bray not! here comes Tukā, the servant of Vishṇu. These donkeys do not know whom they ought to rise before and respect. Tukā is a lion to evil doers, but dust on the feet of the saints.

VII.—His Sense of Authority and Assurance

2733

IN solitary and crowded places we shall raise this cry; there is no particle of pollution here. We have authority both to give and to take, we see no other to call us to account. I have the key of the treasury; you may see here whatever article you need. Tukā says, God has set us here in freedom, by reason of our faith.

2734

WHATEVER duties I have propounded spring from my own experience; what has Pānduranga left wanting? Tukā says, The name of Rāma Kṛishṇa is sweet, the object of our fond desires; let us weave a garland of it.

2735

LET people praise or blame me as they will, and say I have lost my reason. My own rule is to think of what I aim at; why should I defer to men? Tukā says, Why should I join in the fabrications of the world? Any pleasure given by worldly life is fleeting.

2736

I SPEAK inspired words, uttering a message from God; let no one give Shame a place. This vile creature has destroyed the good paths to salvation, and led all mankind on the road that leads to Yama. She has established herself in the common intercourse of men; her treacherous nature no one knows. Tukā says, Bring her to the temple, I will put her to shame and dismiss her.

2737

I LAID aside fear; this is how I reached this spot, where I can entreat thee close at hand. With the power of authority, I shall ask thee to feed me; up till now, I have made this my own care. I have preyed upon my vitals to get me this butter; who would entreat piteously for a trifle? Tukā says, This coarse millet mixed with milk I do not want; you are teasing me with unrealities, O Pānduranga!

2738

WE shall speak with a view to being useful, as opportunity arises, according to the case. We shall lay the foundations deep and build a wall that will not sink, wherein God is first, midmost, and last. What we have to do, we shall do at once; if we rely on the future, the growth of the present will be stunted. Tukā says, We shall obey his orders; we shall carry them out at a single stroke.

2739

THESE are no borrowed words, no worthless chaff meant to amuse men. I have a close train of experiences; they are never far from me. What is needed is something with a flavour; what use are insipid words? Tukā says, Who would take any interest in a man who lurks behind ashamed?

VIII.—Consolation and Happiness in God

2740

WHAT I conceived in my mind appears now before my eyes; I have compassed all that I aimed at, my longing has borne fruit.

2741

FOR many days I forget this path; now I have followed it, and all my grief has been chased away. Long I was devoted to the world and its shows; now I have freed myself from the ways of men. Tukā says, Here I have found courage; my spirit is at peace in the joy of the Highest.

2742

MY sitting, sleeping, and eating are in Govinda; the three words are filled with joy. The course of time has parted me from all things; I have not leisure enough for my needs. I have apportioned every member of my body to its elements, so that nothing of this kind can interfere with me. This divine form has proved an acceptable dish; other fancies have vanished. Wrath and lust destroy the mind and reason; it is peace that swallows up the eddying whirl of error. My mind says, Tukā, is dyed for ever in the dye of Shriranga.

2743

I AM not strong enough to bear the weight of knowledge; my fixed resolution is just to offer service to my Lord. I am determined to repose on obedience to him; this assuredly will set me free from all burdens. We persist in our childish importunities; our father and mother will have to do as we ask. Tukā says, This is the fashion of my service; all my burden has been placed on God.

2744

IN the deep sea of bliss the waves are of bliss; in the body of bliss every member is of bliss. How can I describe what has happened? It is something extraordinary; the course of delight can go no further. The desires of the unborn child show themselves in the longings of the mother, his wishes are reflected there. Tukā says, There is an impression printed on me, and the words that come to my lips are cast in the same mould.

2745

I FIND the whole world dreary; no one knows me for a friend. I am dismayed as I look on the hosts of wild beasts; no courage is left me. I cannot go forward a step in the darkness; I feel sure the thorns will pierce me. All alone, without a companion, I am come to a spot where the road breaks up; I am sorely afraid; I dare not walk on. Tukā says, My good guide shows me the way, and yet he continues to stand apart from me.

2746

I WILL not study or repeat any other words; our one sufficing spell is Pānduranga. I will neither wander about, nor shut myself up, but I will repair to the throng of Vishnu's worshippers. I know nothing else, I practise no austerities; I dance with sleepless eyes amid the train of pilgrims. I observe neither fast nor vow nor fulfilment of vows. I know not, says Tukā, how to serve or praise any other than Rāma Krishna.

2747

WHEN people have once squared their accounts, they all feel quite relieved; no one can lord it over any one then. Every one gets what is due to him, and every one is satisfied; joy and sorrow are both done with. When a transaction is over, each party retires naturally into himself; if any point of difference arises, then there is an occasion for speech. Tukā has settled up his accounts, he stands clear of all complications; so now he has nothing to talk about but the sweet theme of peace.

2748

I HAVE grown like a lump of dough, all plump and straight upstanding. There are no hollows in me anywhere; I put on a fresh colour every day.

I have found a patron; I have escaped from my load of earth. All quarters of the earth are open to me; I have no round of toil to go through. I roll at the doors of the temple; the gadflies all fly away from me. I will not brook a load; Tukā has grown a rich and mighty man. Look at him at the temple-door, he wears a cloak of rags.

2749

I PASS along a road where one escapes from 'Do this' and 'Don't do that'; I keep company with the saints. The saints have reared the first of their flags; at the sight of that sign I shout aloud Hari's name. Tukā says, Come along this road; be assured that Pānduranga will meet you.

2750

I WILL tell you now with what emulation, with what determination I drink this juice. Even as an ant devours sugar, whatever difficulties you put in her way, even so is it with my soul; I cannot leave the feet of Keshāva. The desire for sensuous objects is a field I will not cultivate. When a hungry dog meets food, he barks his life out; but he does not relinquish the morsel in his mouth. What do we mean by a mind subdued? An impassioned man looks on his life as straw; a paramour runs after her lover; such is Tukā's devotion to God.

2751

I CAN see no wicked man anywhere; no one in the universe but my father and mother. Since this is so, why should I fret or fear or vex myself with care? I am entrusted to the care of him who feeds the world; the saints lead me by their own paths.

2752

AS when a famine-stricken man searching for food comes across a dainty meal, even so is it with my mind when it sees thy feet. When a cat sees a pat of clotted cream it sits still with its eyes fixed upon it; even so, says Tukā, my mind thinks of pouncing on thy feet.

2753

THE impulses of my mind were stilled, the energy of action was crippled within me, a sign from within was bestowed on me. My eyes were flushed and half-closed, my throat choked, my hair stood on end. My mind was dazzled by the primal form before me, my joy was such that it could not stir forth. A dawn of purple splendour broke upon me, I drank a draught of life-giving nectar. My soul was waved round the sun and moon, wave after wave of joy came rolling in. Tukā says, I rocked to and fro with joy and love, I lost all conscious sense.

2754

EARTHLY rays are various, red, white, black and yellow, but the unguent of intelligence has entered my eyes. By the virtue of this unguent I have acquired the sight of God; the notions of unity and duality have left me. Differences of space and time, differences of objects have disappeared, the soul is assured that its true form is the universe. There is no such thing as the world; all is the highest Bramhā, I recognize that I am He. The knowledge that thou art He, the joy of complete union with Bramhā, that has now entered into Tukā.

2755

IN the Stainless One I have established my home; in the Formless One I abide. In the unconscious I dwell serene; I have obtained to unbroken unity. Tukā says, No sense of self is left in me; I have taken the form of the divine, I am for ever pure.

IX.—Admonitions to himself

2756

HOW can a man be ruined if he remembers thee, and is moreover a servant of Vishnu? True, we are sometimes driven to despair in the world, yet I have earnestly followed after thee. What I have seized, I will now carefully discriminate; I will not suffer my mind to lose hold of it. Tukā says, I cannot be lost for ever; this the Puranas proclaim.

2757

I HAVE often resolved not to speak to the world; but then some sin stands upright across my way, and my mood changes. I have set my neck free from the world; how is it then misfortunes overtake me? They interrupt thy service, says Tukā; how can I help this, O Pāndu-ranga?

2758

WHAT I want, is to incur the ridicule of the world; then I shall never leave thy feet, for my mind in its distress will seek its own proper place. I do not enough abhor idle talk; I know not why such vile promptings arise in me. Tukā says, Only, if I am dealt a stout blow on the head, shall I cease from these vanities.

2759

I HAVE grown sick of my own lot in the world; what do I care about social rules of conduct? I have neither kin nor friends beside God. These ears of mine listen to no talk of worldly affairs; my mind is grown weary of them. Tukā says, Show me what favour Thou wilt, but do not hold me, to no purpose, in the bonds of pleasure and pain.

2760

SPEAK to me no more of the world; I will listen to no speech but speech of God. When a man has achieved prosperity, who will scrutinize his merits or demerits? But all the possessions I acquired, from long ago till to-day, thieves have stolen from me. Only when the leaves are pruned off can we expect a crop. Tukā will have no huge error left to entangle him.

2761

SO long as I have been under your power, so long I have been in disgrace; now I will not let you stay in this country, so powerful a master I have found. When did this snake approach me in my childhood? I knew not how sinful thou art? Tukā says, I have done with this traffic now; I mean to lay thee low.

2762

I WILL unite myself at least a little with this image of thyself; I will acquaint myself with thy feet, then do thou as thou wilt. By an effort of my body, I will offer thee Ganges water and a tulsi leaf. Tukā says, I fold my hands—this is all the service I can render thee.

2763

FRAME no purposes of thy own, O mind; fix thy thoughts on these feet of Viṭṭhobā. His holy face is moulded out of joy; grief and folly and pain are not to be seen there. You will find rest there, says Tukā; all earthly hopes for the future will pass away.

2764

WHY should I feel shy? I have laid aside hesitation and opened my mouth. Here, on earth, no notice is taken of a dumb creature; no real good can be secured by over-modesty. Such words as occur to me I address to my lord; I embolden my soul and pass straight on. Tukā says, O mind of mine, you have to wrestle with the powerful; slap your thighs and stand forward.

2765

I WILL lay at the feet of God all my powers and any misery that may overtake me. My voice will not henceforth find room to express any other feelings. The distraction of my mind, the chaos of my reason, the repentance I feel, may continue as they were. Tukā says, I will set my affections on Viṭṭhobā; the root of joy shall wax strong within me.

2766

O MIND, why do you trust so much the wet clay of your body? Your eyes, handsome and clearly outlined as they are, old age will turn into cotton seeds. Your nose, handsome and straight as it is, will come down to meet your chin. Tukā says, While death is not yet at hand, show some regard to Hari.

2767

SIT well inside your shop, listening and meditating; when you see customers arrive, empty out your sacks of good and bad. Don't foolishly puff out your cheeks; keep a full stock of goods. Hold the scales fairly; make no fraudulent sales. Tukā is turned a grocer; he avoids the eighty-four lakhs of lives.

2768

I AM resolved in my mind to have no discussions with men; I would attain my own purpose; this design I would set before myself and steadily adhere to it. What use to me are the notions of others? Am I not Viṭṭhobā's worshipper? There are a few who have gone ahead to show the way; why should I foolishly quit that way? Tukā says, Viṭṭhobā undertakes all anxiety for me; I need not fear.

2769

SET no sinful desire before my eyes; better I were blind! Let my ears listen to no scandal; make me rather deaf, O God! Let me never lust after other men's wives; better this clay were removed from the earth! Tukā says, I abhor everything; I find my pleasure in Gopāla alone.

X.—Some incidents in his life

2770

HOW is it this time of trouble has overtaken me? To-day I have been afflicted; I was harassed in the hour of God's service. It is through some sin of mine, and through the visit of these people. Tukā says, They came to pour wicked words into my ears.

2771

HE will not let me sleep in the morning, and at night he keeps on twittering like a sparrow. This wretch is ever at my back, turning my life into torment. He brings with him a crowd of people, and sits at his ease in the temple. So here I am come to my own house, says Tukā, to fall into the horrors of my wife's mouth.

2772

THEY will light a firebrand and ruin me. There is a crowd pressing in upon me; I am caught in a ravine of the hills. They will find out a weak point in me, and attack me. Tukā says, The crowd is so dense that I cannot go forward.

2773

I HAVE come to understand what I understood not; therefore instead of speech I practise silence. Since once we met, you and I are parted. Now I do not fondly look forward to meeting you. Tukā says, My single-minded faith has put an end to pilgrimage to and fro.

2774

ASK Pānduranga for the things you desire; why besiege a feeble creature like me? This is why I retired from the world; delusive desires grow upon us without end. Whatever we do, we cannot find peace; when we reflect, we find a holy rite to be sinful. Tukā says, 'Twere well now to remain quite still, and remember thee, O Pānduranga.

2775

SHOULD we give thee up now, we have nothing in our hand or knotted up in our dress; our friends and kindred have forsaken us. So far as the world goes, I am become like dry leaves blown about by the wind; so I have lost all shame. I dare not go to any one's door; I have brought this degradation on myself. What false step did my mind take? I can find no refuge now. Tukā says, You have many worshippers, so there is no room for me here.

2776

I THROW me down and roll on the ground within thy court-yard; sprinkle holy water on me. My body will grow moist and root; it is racked by the manifold fever of life. When shall I reach this spot, I asked myself; by chance I came in time for the leavings thy food. Tukā says, Report, some one, my presence in the temple; Pānduranga will approach me.

2777

WHAT can I do? This passion has seized my boy; he is always going to the temple. He will not listen to anything else that you tell him; his mind is full of Viṭṭhobā. He will not follow his trade at home; he is always dispirited there. Nothing of the kind was ever known in our family; we never had a madman like him. He pays no attention to what people say; he has become a stranger to me. Tukā says, These are the words of wicked men; they will go to hell.

2778

YOU are my protector, but these clowns cannot perceive this. They revile me face to face, and behind my back; they will some day go to hell. They call me a poet, though in their sinful hearts they deny it. Tukā says, Who would pay any heed now to this world?

2779

WHERE shall I find food? Whom shall I go to? Under whose protection shall I stay in this town? The headman here has censured the town's people; who will give me a morsel now? The people says, he has lost all sense of decency; they drag me before the court. Respectable people have brought the matter before the headman; I am a feeble creature; they have ruined me. Tukā says, Their company is not good for me; I shall go now to seek Viṭṭhobā.

2780

A DENSE crowd of Ḥari's worshippers is assembled; there is no room to enter even the skirts of it. What can I do there? Who will listen to what I say? How can I rebuke you for this, when I too call myself your worshipper? I know not how to clap the cymbals nor to dance in time. They are decked with splendid ornaments, my body is in wretched plight. Tukā says, O consort of Kamalā, do not make me subject to these men!

2781

IN earlier days, I took up many amusements; my energy is now all spent. I can neither move nor take a step; my body is emptied of all its strength. It is like a fold of cloth that has been burnt; a strip of cloth that cannot bear pulling. Tukā says, The moment you try to touch it, it will cover the world with ashes.

2782

TO-DAY a Manga has touched me, and polluted my person. I will undergo the penance meet for this, filling my heart with Viṭṭhobā. When rage encounters me, he makes me vomit filth out of my mouth. I will now bathe in penitence, says Tukā, and look upon the sun.

2783

WITHIN fifteen days I saw his form visibly; the formless Viṭṭhobā met my gaze. Know that I made my dwelling on the top of mount Bhamba; I made steady the impulses of my mind in the highest Bramhā. Viewing the hour as my last, I sat down in a steady posture, and began to meditate on the divine. Snakes, scorpions, and tigers beset and assailed me. As camphor disappears in a flame, so did my body disappear, says Tukā.

2784

THIS ignorant body was merged in the primal form; it was overtaken by dissolution. I attained the primal form of enlightenment; the flame of knowledge was kindled within me. Tukā says, My mind remained in the primal form; my body found rest at thy feet.

2785

WE go now to our own village; receive our 'Rama, Rama'. You and we shall not meet again; hereafter, the chain of our rebirth will be broken. Cease to pity me, I entreat you. Are any of you coming to your true home with me? If so, call on the name of Viṭṭhobā. Utter the name of Rāma Krishṇa; I Tukā go to Vaikunṭha.

XI.—His mode of life

2786

I OFFER salutations to God; this is my principle; what do ablutions cost me? I sweep the road before the saints, no matter whether it brings me loss or gain. Whether *you* do it or not, to do it is my fond desire; for I love devotion and I have nothing else to do. I offer service to God, I preach, I dance in the temple court; I enjoy the bliss of love to the full. Tukā says, I desire not liberation; this mortal life is sweet to me when I receive it.

2787

BODY, mind, and possessions I have surrendered to the Lord of Pāndhari; no greed after money, no anxious cares, no hopes reside in me now; I have loosed off me the net of worldly interests. Tukā says, I carry with me only the name of Viṭṭhobā and not a copper of money.

2788

'EMPLOY me to perform a *kathā*'—if I say so to any one, let my tongue rot away from me. *Thou* art my helper; what is there lacking with thee? What need I ask from other creatures? Tukā says, All powers reside in thy feet.

2789

I WILL be born as one of the pebbles sharp or round, the particles of dust large or small, on the road to Pāndhari; I shall touch the feet of the saints. I will be born as hosen or sandals, on the feet of any of the saints; as a cat or dog or hog, to lick up the food they leave. As a drain or step or stream or well on the Ganges' bank, for the saints walk across them. Set me, O God, in any place where the feet of the saints will touch me.

2790

WHERE is no place in me now for sin or merit, for anxiety about loss or gain; living, I am dead; 'My Own' and 'Other's' have vanished; the root of worldly cares is cut through. Rank, race, colour, creed and caste; all are gone; there is room no more for truth or falsehood. Life among men, life in the forest, the active life, the inactive, they are the same with me; I cannot find any difference between one thing and another. Tukā says, When I offered my body to Viṭṭhobā, I did all that was needed to worship him.

2791

SOME respect I do show men, according as I think proper; otherwise prince and peasant are alike. I am indifferent to my own person; so there is no fear or preference in me. Tukā says, I amuse myself with unforced diversion; I am therefore above joy or grief.

2792

GIVE me not learning nor life lasting through length of days; I am not mad after liberation. Let me die uttering 'Rama Krishna,'—this is the gift I ask of thy grace. Give me not wealth or honour; let no children be born to me. Let me die with the name of Nārāyana on my lips. This, says Tukā, is my prayer, O Pānduranga!

2793

WHAT loss will you suffer, if you accept my service without an agreement as to wages? What wages need you pay me? I string together rhymes and preach eccentric doctrines; I have no true knowledge or spirit of devotion. My speech is incapable of expressing thy attributes; I put forth such arguments as will put others to silence. So keep me at your feet, and *then* you will see some spirit of love in me. People will laugh at you, says Tukā, because you insist that your worshippers should have no desire.

XII.—His relation with the Saints

2794

THE saints have raised me to eminence, as a jujube tree is pervaded by the sandal trees that surround it. They never asked about my faults or merits or caste; they gave me a place at their feet. Tukā says, If a man can please a rich and powerful patron, a beggar is turned into a prince.

2795

I WILL carry on my shoulders the sandals and hosen of the saints; I will dance before them with the cymbals in my hand. I know nothing of the ritual of worship or means of attainment; of mystic contemplation, meditation, postures, trance; I am ignorant, unashamed, I cannot recognize musical notes. All my possessions, family and treasure, says Tukā, are the feet of saints and teachers.

2796

AFTER much length of time, my merit bore fruit; good fortune dawned and left its impression. How is it it came to meet me? I reached the feet of the saints. Now vanished are my eager longings, the fetters cast upon me by the misery of life; I see manifest before me the eternal Bramhā, purple in hue. My body was glorified by the embrace of the saints, when I laid my head at their feet. Tukā says, I am fully satisfied with the bliss the saints have bestowed on me; I fell prostrate when I saw their troop before me.

2797

IN future lives, bring me to life in the houses of Hari's servants. If you bid me ask for something, then I say 'Grant me this, O Pānduranga!' When I throw myself at the saints' feet, be not ashamed. Give me strength, says Tukā; I will dance in their joyous assemblies.

XIII.—Tukā's Brother

2798

WHAT shall I say, O Lord of the senses? Such a fit of remorse has passed over me that I cannot wait a moment to swallow you up? You have ruined my house; you have sent my poor children begging from door to door; you have parted them and set them wailing. All I can do now is to take your life and give you mine, for my brother's sake. Whether the world call me good or bad, says Tukā's brother, *that* shall not make me quit my hold on you.

2799

WHEN my father and mother died, I was left to depend on my brother; yet even then, O Hari, you gave us no help. Is this the return you make for devotion, to destroy a prosperous household? Is this the end of the transaction, is this the grace you dealt in? Hanging on one life were two families; could you dare, O shameless wretch, to disorder it? Tukā's brother says, What else can we call you? He was a madman to join himself to you.

2800

WE heard long ago that this befell our forefathers; O consort of Shri, thou didst make them thy servants and set them free from all anxious care. Why dost thou pursue us thus, why is it even now thou hast not ceased; how long wilt thou try us? We have a quarrel with thee from life to life; why dost thou keep up the same pretence? How is it, says Tukā's brother, thou art become so blind? One who eats not cannot bear to see one who eats.

2801

WE were managing our affairs prosperously; we were filling our bellies; you brought upon us this Spirit of Mischief; you displayed your divine power. Why did you utterly destroy our family? We were the only branches that were left; yet you could not bear to see even us; you put an open estrangement between us. Tukā's brother says, Because you found the top of the cane sweet, need you eat it up root and all?

2802

YOU understand full well what right and wrong are; therefore you can produce night by closing your own eyes. Answer me now as best you can; I have woven a net round you. Of set purpose, you have made yourself ignorant, the better to enjoy the service of men; yet this conviction will bear fruit for him alone who holds it. Tukā's brother says, Now no one can blame us; it is you who have made us cling to your feet.

2803

SHOULD any misery overtake our children, bethink thee what the result will be, O Infinite One. We have reached tranquillity, without pains in speech or word; we have escaped from drudgery and fatigue. We have penetrated your secret and got you comfortably in our grasp. You can make no excuse for yourself. Tukā's brother says, You have cheated me finely; move on before me, fellow, I have had the good luck to secure you.

2804

O GOD, you owe a debt to my forefathers; why haven't you paid it off to me yet? Your turbulence has brought you into notice; be assured I shan't let you sneak away safe and sound. I shall make the whole affair known; I shall produce you before the saints; why need I be afraid of you when I am asking for my own? I was an ignorant child till now; you improved on the opportunity; now I will not abate one *cowri* of my rights. Tukā's brother says, I have already drowned my soul in water; I shall tie my throat fast to your feet.

2805

HAD I known you well in the past, I should not have let you take breath; I should have forced you to a settlement there and then. Had I not been so backward, I should not have had to wait so long; what need was there to bring a closed transaction before a court? Though our commodities were genuine, how often we had to call on you and go away! My brother sat thirteen days at your door. Even at this late hour, O Hari, avoid the censure of the world; else, says Tukā's brother, you will have no vestige of honour left.

2806

I WILL not wait a moment; I know your reputation. I will not let you stir without doing something for me. With whom have you to deal? Why do you close your eyes? I will take you before the court; yield! or I will drag you there. You give nothing willingly, I know, as long as we are quiet and do no mischief; yet we have begun by making this request to you. How many you have ruined in this way! There is no end to their number. I, Tukā's brother, say, you will now give up this way of yours.

2807

MY brother has gained a treasure which countless ages cannot exhaust; at one onslaught he has brought down the whole of Vaikuṇṭha. There is no more coming and going for us, nothing more for us to do; life after life we may sit and feast comfortably. This treasure cannot be counted; it fills the heavens with joy, the whole earth is continually filled with it. Tukā's brother says, A marvellous treasure of the highest bliss we have found.

XIV.--Descriptions and Invocations

2808

O EVIL age I fear thee not, for I love dearly this name. Thou knowest not who it is that strengthens me; it is Nārāyana, the help of the saints. He slew Shankha in the ocean, and came back with the four Vedas. In the form of the Tortoise, he slew the mighty demon, and hid his hands and feet under his belly. In the form of the great Boar, did he valiantly sustain the earth on his tusk. He tore Hiranyakoshipa and protected Pralhada; he became a Dwarf, and cast the demon Bali down into hell. He lopped off the thousand arms and brought back the cow of wishes. His prowess made stones float on the sea; he slew Ravana and set Bibhishma on the throne. When the enemy began to vex Panchali, Hari made himself into clothes. Tukā says, All who have become one in form with Hari have not returned to birth again.

2809

THE gods and the demons churned the ocean, thus a burden was laid on the earth that it could not bear. Then didst thou become a tortoise and hold it on thy back; thou dost take thought for all, O Hari! Then did all the gods offer their praises. There are countless such stories of thee, says Tukā; he of the thousand tongues was wearied in reciting them.

2810

IN this wise did Durvāsa bring the message back; then, O Nārāyana, didst thou grow in stature. Thou didst set thy feet at Bali's gate, thou didst lengthen out the head on thy trunk, thou didst force an entrance into Dvaravati, and make thy way out. Hence, says Tukā, did that place become known as Dvāraka.

2811

THOU didst slay the two demons Maru and Kushan; thou didst make Durvāsa, the Lord of sages, happy.

2812

VOID of talent as I am how can I describe thy imagined form, when the Vedas and Shrutis are silent concerning it? I have made for thee an ornament of my mind; I have set thy lotus feet in my heart. Thy holy face is moulded out of happiness; it dispels my thirst and hunger. My tongue delights to sing these verses, my spirit is pacified. Tukā says, I gaze upon thy feet, thy lovely feet with saffron dyed.

2813

THY glory is incomprehensible, the Vedas close their mouths before it; the mind and the breath are foot-sore before they overtake it. From thee sun and moon derive their light; what is my reason in such a matter? How can I describe thy splendour? The serpent with a thousand tongues cannot sufficiently praise thee. We are thy children, says Tukā, thou art our mother; O spread over us the shade of thy mercy!

XV.—Pandhari and Vitthoba

2814

GO, go to Pandhari; be, be a pilgrim there! Would you leave the pebbly shore for Vaikunṭha? Load your shoulders with flags, put tulsi wreaths and powder on yourselves. In the crowded gathering of saints, Tukā falls on the ground.

2815

PUNDALIKA is the Prince of devotees, he has achieved his aim, he has brought his own highest Bramha from Vaikunṭha. Pānduranga in the image of a child, along with the cows and cowherds, comes before us out of love and stands upright and unmoved. Truly this is another Vaikunṭha, with one letter prefixed to it; men may talk of other places, but they are not like this. Within a circuit of ten miles round the place sin cannot enter; how then can there be any question of actions prescribed or forbidden? The Purānas affirm that the people there are gods with four hands. It rests on the holy wheel, so that no enemy can enter there throughout a whole age. Pandhari is great among holy places, its glory is unrivalled. Blessed, blessed, says Tukā, are the pilgrims that go there.

2816

THE bliss of Vaikunṭha has visited Pandhari; Pundalika has stored it all up. Take it, take it, my good friends; make your tongue the true measure of it. Make but one journey hither; you need never make another. Roll up and lay aside the impressive shows of the world; as long as lasts your little life, dwell in Pandhari. Neglect not this gain; Tukā entreats the country folk.

2817

TO be endowed with all attributes is a mark of this God alone; others have some of them one, some another. The six divine perfections exist in the Supreme alone; Tukā says, Whatever you can name is found as a grace in this Viṭṭhala.

2818

THIS satisfies the longings of our sense; we shall find it sweeter as time goes on. The best use of our life upon earth is to visit Pandharpur. We shall see with our eyes that source of bliss; it will settle in the very base of our mind. Tukā says, Our ears will judge of the samples they hear and present us with the good.

2819

THE market day when *Ashādha* is near; the market day in *Kartika*; these two are enough, you need not trade on other days. This is what you should buy and sell; a heap of union with God accompanied by faith. I know of nothing and nobody, says Tukā, but Viṭṭhobā.

2820

HA! Pundalika! what made you so insolent, that you set Viṭṭhala standing upright here? How came you to be so rude, that you threw a brick behind you? Full eight and twenty ages have now passed, but you do not say 'Sit down!' Seeing your ardent faith, God left Vaikunṭha; you are indeed, O Pundalika, says Tukā, a sturdy fellow!

2821

THIS is an ancient mine we have opened up; though rifled by many hands it is not exhausted. Sages and masters and adepts have preserved it with care. It became known through the virtue of a child born feet foremost; Pundalika proclaimed it to the world. Tukā says, I was present here as a poor man, I was lucky enough to get a portion of it small or large.

2822

BLESSED are they that live in Pandhari, blessed are these creatures that they were born; all that belong to the four kingdoms of life, insects and royal birds alike, possessed of the three qualities. Castes high and low, men, women and children, they have all of them become four-armed gods. Tukā says, I will be born and dwell there; I will be a neglected stone of Pandhari.

2823

AS for those who say that Bramha is different from Viṭṭhala, let not the saints pay any heed to their words. Any other worship than that of Viṭṭhala, be assured, is all a delusion. Whoever tell tales of any other than Viṭṭhala, be assured, their countenances shall fall. Whatever knowledge they have save knowledge of Viṭṭhala, all that learning is wasted. Tukā says, Viṭṭhala alone is true, all else is an impressive sham.

2824

A MAN should seize a piece of good luck ready to his hand; he should store up such goods as will not come to an end. A store of goods has come to Pandharpur; they have been sold on credit at a profit. Empty now your bags and fill them in haste with this commodity. Tukā says, Like the saints, we too shall spread forth our cloaks.

2825

THE infinite Veda has spoken, but this is all the purport brought to light; we should seek the protection of Viṭṭhobā, we should sing his name with fixed attention. The deliberations of the Shastras has settled only this. This creed, says Tukā, is the conclusion of the eighteen Purānas.

2826

I LOVE the town of Pandhari, the Bhima, Pānduranga, the Chandrabhāga, the linga and Pundalika.

2827

HAPPY are they who dwell in Pandhari; their speech is sweet, their bodies are glorified; the dull, the feeble-minded, the thoughtless, the wicked, at Pandhari they are full of compassion. All are full of peace and forbearance, forgetful of the world, free from desire and stain of impurity. They have no pride of caste, says Tukā, they are all emancipated souls.

2828

A PILLAR of wisdom he made himself, hence his name is Viṭṭhobā. How is it you know not his name? Is it not known to the Veda? The serpent set forth his praise, but his tongue was riven and he became nothing but a bed for him to lie on. Tukā says, His authority prevails over the head of Time.

2829

WHOSO has gone to Pandharpur he contemplates no other pilgrimage. Accessible is the prince of Pandhari, my mother; she attends to the signs which our souls make to her. He who has a heap of merits from past lives, he does well to go to Pandharpur. When we leave it we feel ready to die, our throat is choked with sobs. They say, 'Finish the meal of holy curds; turn your face back to it once more. Let us see the place again, and catch sight of the Lord of Pandhari.' Tūkā says, O very heaven upon earth is the pebbly bank of the Bhima!

2830

PUNDALIKA brought down to earth the Lord of Vaikunṭha; he was eminently blessed. He was the strength of fortitude, the crown of worshippers, unblemished in faith, the sanctifier of merit. Through the merit gained by serving his parents he obtained a treasure; the eternal Bramha embraced him. Yea, he spent a time of joy and mirth with him; for know that there came to his house a guest from Vaikunṭha. Blessed was his glorious strength, his devotion known to all men. Tukā says, Liberation lies suppliant at his feet.

2831

IN my first verse I shall weave the three worlds together and sing of holy Pānduranga. In my second I say there is no second to him; in the wilderness and in resorts of men Pānduranga meets me. In my third verse, I say there is no particle of mere matter anywhere, all is God. In my fourth, I put my grain into the mill; I sing my treasure Pānduranga. In my fifth, I sing Pānduranga, my mother's home for ever. In my sixth, the six shastras close, Pānduranga comes forward to be my teacher. In my seventh, I remember Pānduranga every moment, he is seated before my eyes. My eighth reminds me that for twenty-eight ages Pānduranga has stood on the Chandrabhāga. With my ninth the grinding ceases, I escape death while I am still in the world. This is my tenth, O ten times incarnate, Tukā prays, may I never return to this life again.

2832

IN proof of this their arms are raised; consult the Vedas and the Purāṇas.

2833

THIS player on the Bhima stage, he has altogether bewitched me. My mind and my reason are stupefied, they have lost their skill in worldly affairs. How conformably to the occasion he speaks; with what courtesy he lays his restraints upon us! A great enchanter is he, says Tukā; he stands waiting for us everywhere.

2834

COME let us go to Alandi and look on Dnyāndeva.

2835

DAMOJI PANT sent off his cash balance; God saved him from shame. Attend, all of you, listen to the tale; I make my salutation to the saints. He was dwelling at Mangalvedha with his family, a man honoured by all the traders there. What was his vocation? He was headman of the district, when a famine occured there; he broke open the royal granaries and saved Pandhari from famine; poor wretches who had none to help them he rescued, and his fame spread throughout the kingdom. The accountant was a Kanarese Bramhana, he sent in a complaint. The unbored[1] who ruled at Bedar, when he saw the paper summoned Damoji. Damoji was arrested and sent off.—Come here! see how Viṭṭhala deceived them! He raised the current price by a quarter, and put down as much money as all the grain was worth. He wrote a report in Damoji's name, put it in the sack and sealed it up. Then Viṭṭhala came to the help of his worshippers, he made himself a Mahāra; he went to the king at Bedar. 'Johāra!' he cried. The prince, his father and mother, ask 'Whence come you?' 'My home is at Mangalvedha,' says he. 'Damoji has sent you the cash balance.' He emptied the sack and poured out the report. The king was glad to see it; he says 'I need not have summoned him.' 'What is your name?' say the clerks; 'I am Vithā the porter,' says he, 'let the prince give a receipt for the money.' 'We will count it out and give you

[1] Unbored. This is a term of reproach used by a Hindu towards a Mussalman.

one,' say they. They wrote and gave him a receipt: the king gave him leave to depart. An umbrella, a horse, a litter he sent with him and a messenger to accompany him. Now they missed Damoji on the road as they went back, and they all reached Mangalvedha as they were. Damoji was taken to Bedar; the prince says 'I am amazed to see you! Yesterday Vithā the porter came with the money; I gave him leave to depart and sent an answer with him. Say at once what do you want? Tell me your purpose.' 'How did Vithā come here? Who sent him? When?' They brought out the record and laid it before him. When he saw it his heart was broken, his eyes filled with tears and he turned to the king. 'My lord, my lord, I will be your servant no more; you have wearied my friend Viṭṭhobā.' He took leave and went to his own place; he turned his back on the world henceforth. Thus did Damoji serve Pandhari, Hari stood close by him as a servant. Tukā says, Vittho is the champion of those that have no protector; Hari does not disappoint his servants.

2836

THE spirit which none could control was nailed by Pundalika to this spot.

2837

THE final truth of the *sutras* is that God alone exists, but Pānduranga is a sea of mercy. 'Hari—Om' with rising and falling tones of inflection is all comprised in Pānduranga. Though he belongs not to the three high castes, he is the very source of the Veda, says Tukā.

IV

The Nature of God

I.—In Himself

2838

THE Shrutis say of him 'Not that, not that'; Tukā says, His own essential form is the seed from which reality springs.

2839

CAN we or how can we comprehend thee? How can we bring thee within our experience? Whether thou hast or hast not attributes, whether thou art great or small I can form no idea. How can I resolve, what plan can I form to cross the sea of the world? Tukā says, How can we reach thy feet? I know not the secret.

2840

WE are but simple and faithful worshippers, how can we fathom your propensities? We heard of your grandeur and approached you with a prayer. Though you truly exist, you have become here as though you were not; our eager desires do but multiply our anxieties. Hitherto, with all our reflection, we cannot comprehend you; without patience we shall lose all our pains. Tukā says, Speech has led to further speech, my intelligence has grown keen.

2841

I FEEL compelled to sing of God and worship him; as a stranger in a strange land I cannot be silent. He recognizes no elder or younger; no power second to himself. From the very beginning he needed no relative or mother. As chance presented itself he forsook them all, but through the impulse of love he set on foot a plan for uniting others with himself. The Supreme Soul was corrupted by becoming an individual soul; he was melted and poured into several moulds. In his desire for ornaments he turned himself into baser metal—how could his properties be distinguished? Now while the metal is still molten, better it were to make the whole a glittering mass. We cannot discern its true nature without hammering it; Tukā is impatient to do so; I will disclose what was in my mind. Inspire me with a keen desire to begin; then I will sing thy praise.

II.—His relation to the world

2842

IF you bring it to pass, this may happen: the dull may grow sharp, and the learned mad. Yet no one knows the secret; I prefer to endure the pits of sorrow. A lame man can cross a mountain, a dumb man can speak, a sinful man grow virtuous, a wicked man abstain from injuries, all this can Hari bring to pass in mere sport, he can set the whole world free. He amuses himself, says Tukā; he observes the world, pervading it yet sitting apart.

2843

THE mind is nothing but the act of thinking, which follows the lusts of the senses as they grow. As the body makes progress, the hands and feet are apparently separate, but the soul controls all. Light belongs entirely to the sun, though in speech we give different names to it under different forms. Tukā says, From speech proceeds the measure of difference; if we keep silence how can we distinguish between various aspects of things?

2844

DOES our attendance on you cause a loss to your purse? Why do you keep me aloof by your illusions? You are chief among the wise. O answer me this precisely. What pleasure do you find in this diversion, while we suffer many kinds of pain? Tukā says why do you render yourself void of attributes? Who will save us now?

2845

GOD is wise; he puts forth all his authority in a moment of time. God is skilful; he acts with full knowledge of our hearts. God is separate from the world, from all taint of pollution, says Tukā.

2846

YOUR body belongs to God, your wealth to Kubera; what right has man over these things? It is God who gives and brings about all gifts, who leads and causes us to be led; what power has man in these matters? Yet this mortal creature esteems himself master of the cause; he wastes his life saying 'Mine', 'Mine' Tukā says, To secure perishable treasures, why do you struggle with God.

2847

THOU hast created us and bestowed on us properties; it is fit therefore that thou shouldst protect us. For thyself thou hast no desires in respect of pleasure or pain, but thou shouldst not see thy servants lack anything; thou shouldst give them what they need. Tukā says, O Feeder of the Universe, direct thy glance to what is straight before thee!

2848

WHEN we merge ourselves in the source of all life, the whole of creation appears to us as a form of Hari. Tukā says, What shall I say? By a sudden impulse I am filled with Hari.

2849

THE Feeder of the Universe is present throughout it; life and lifeless things exist through him. In him all find a place; all gods find a refuge in him. Tukā says, Desire no other gods; if you look on them as different from him, guilt instead of merit will cling to you.

2850

WHY do you force yourselves into a madness for religion? God stands just before you. He has neither front nor back, yet he swallows the three worlds at a mouthful. You do not see the opportunities which lie before you; who would lose anything if you did so? Tukā sings of God by the aid of his name; in this matter there is no 'We' and 'You'.

III.—Union with God necessary

2851

THE tall tree is latent in the seed; the seed is the last of the tree. So is it with you and me; we are absorbed in each other. The waves gather on the water; yet the waves are themselves the water. Tukā says, You are the orb, I am the reflection; in their own original source both are merged.

2852

WHEN bound up in the mind it dwells for ever with it, it shines for ever by its own light. The truest union is that within; it admits of no separation. Within the storehouse of memory the universe can be grasped; it is well you should bear ample room for it. Tukā says, This gain you shall have in the innermost recess of your house, if only you do not break the strings of love.

2853

THAT Lord of souls dwells in the souls of all creatures; keep watch from moment to moment in your own abode. He seems to be different from you, but dwells like a seed within you. Tukā says, Know your duty, lay hold of the secret of contemplation.

2854

GIVE me the power to serve thee, O God, then will I not serve the world. This is the chief duty of man; know this, ye that are capable of knowledge. Know that God exists within your minds, in a form corresponding to your faith. Tukā says, We grow mad after that to which we apply ourselves in fond desire.

2855

SOME of us are thy favoured children, elder or younger, so we can never be scorned by thee, we shall always have gentle answers and sweetmeats from thee. We are not deceived into thinking ourselves separate; we have settled ourselves firmly on the basis of all things. We have put thy own ornaments upon us; every decoration we wear. Though we spend this endless treasure, we never exhaust it; this wealth has no bounds; it cannot be counted. Tukā says, We do lovingly entreat thee, and therefore thou hast shown us this gain.

2856

I EMPTIED my body and made a place therein for Pānduranga; it is now an easy matter to cherish and nurture it; what indeed matters the body when I have full faith in him? When 'I' died, this dwelling-place was prepared for him; this lamp was kindled to all eternity. In one instant I became as though I was not; there is no need to say more, says Tukā.

2857

WE should still entertain the fear, that perhaps his feet may be lost to us. If we are parted from God, what use is life to us? What other stranger can we look on as ourself? Tukā says, It matters not whether the world exists or not.

2858

MY own natural character is beyond my control; even if I surrender it to thee, I gain nothing. I have found this out now, O Nārāyana, for the experience of my waking hours does not agree with my dreams. Whatever part I play, it is all outward show; there is no inner union of me and thee. Tukā says, There is no back or front to truth; it is altogether the same in every part.

2859

NOW it is well to enjoy what is left us in our homes. Good and evil do not pass before our eyes; so no distress of mind is possible. Speech multiplies speech,—fruitless chaff and vexation. If we carry our entreaties to God, what he desires from us is service. As long as we are struggling to clear up accounts between us, we can neither go forward nor backward. Tukā says, Now I have found out that all is well as long as we do not feel ourselves other than God.

2860

THE sea rises up in vapour; then he joins the Ganges and other streams; he is still only sporting with himself. Between the two manifestations what takes place is of no account; it is all the effect of his environment upon him. So it is with you and me. Our vessels and our dwellings are all in the womb of space; they are brought into existence by words, by words they are destroyed. Tukā says, The seed brings forth the seed; fruits and flowers appear and disappear.

2861

HERE and now it is true, that I cannot turn back again. Let any strait come upon me that will; the body brings real things to pass and I am its victim. To find union with thee, we must surrender thee our own souls, O God. Tukā is no designing knave; let us have the case decided in the presence of the four.

2862

WE may close the gates of the senses, but we cannot do away with the disorders they have occasioned; these are incurable. Thou dwellest in the mind, pervading it; it is my view, that thou shouldst be entirely dissociate from objects. There are witnesses of thy grace near us, but mere words accomplish nothing. Tukā says, It is when we actually mingle with thee that we live in harmonious concord; I lie at thy feet and entreat thee for this.

2863

LET no crushing blow fall on me now, for distress would step between us and destroy me. Why did I destroy the soul within me that I felt to be separate from thee? Because my neck was bound by the rope of desire, and I grew quite helpless. Tukā says, I relegate to their own place the tribe of individual souls altogether.

2865

DWELL in a city of cloud-land that lasts but a moment; make that your ancestral home. Weave an invisible chain of sky-flowers, and worship Lakshmī and Nārāyana. Arrange to marry the son of a barren woman, and make haste to gaze on the ceremony. Make a drinking-place of mirage and quench the thirst of heated men of sense. Tukā says, Unreal are our body, our senses and our actions; offer all your actions then to Bramha, good sir, and become Bramha.

2866

PANDURANGA has truly shown us his grace by driving out of us all doubts, all sense of difference from him. A bed is strewn with joy both for my soul and his; we have ascended to a seat above the three worlds. Tukā is laid to rest in the primal form, as a child is lulled by a gentle cradle-song.

2867

WHEN the members of a family pronounce his name to each other, their forefathers, their children, their property are purified. What was declared of old—how can it pass on to the future? He has anointed men with the unction of pure identity. The royal canopy of emancipation gleams on high for an emblem; the sky resounds with unbroken acclamations. The Lord of Tukā sets his servant on his own throne and celebrates a festival of mutual love.

2868

THE life of action, the life of contemplation we have melted into one; we have drawn off a pure extract of both. Our vital activity we have brought low in the fire of grave philosophy, to bring our own soul into union with the highest. Bramha we have cooked in Bramha full speedily; we have found the dish palatable by experience. We have discovered that the two flavours correspond in reaching this end; we have tasted in many mouthfuls contemplation of the self. Tukā attained to good health in his eight members, and showed forth in temple-yards the joy of finding his true self

2869

WITH thee and me it is as with the waves of the sea. There is but one nature between us both. They speak of God and his worshippers as separate only while error has not yet disappeared. As the yarn and the web are one, so is the Pervader one with the universe.

2870

TUKĀ says, In Hari's name my mind passed out of mind.

IV.—Distinction from God necessary

2871

THE ceaseless utterance of thy name has spread far and wide; there is a steady flow of love from thy form. Tukā says, My delight is in devotion; I am in no hurry to be absorbed in God.

2872

If you and I should become one and the same, how then could the service of my Lord exist as a graceful ornament for me to wear? There would be no room for love. If utterance should cease, how could this joy exist? Tukā says, As it is, we dance before thee with fond delight.

2873

WHY should I return to my former course of life, to endure all its struggles? You know this well, O God, but you pay no heed to it; 'twere well if you left me under my present delusion. I broke the very mould of identity with you and escaped from it; but you have allowed indolence to creep over you. Tukā says, Be generous now betimes, there is no reason for long delay.

2874

I HAVE come back to my earlier wish; what I delight in is this bond of servant and master. Give me speedily the gift I have asked for; I still preserve the true principle with me. Of this I avail myself to secure a word from thee; showing this as my passport I shall reach my goal. Tukā says, How many knots must I cut to reach thee, though the sight of thee cuts the knots of the world?

2875

THERE is nothing that my soul desires, but only you, O Keshāva. I seek not Vaikuṇṭha or union with the Absolute; I am well pleased to be born on earth again. Who would desire, for its own sake, this world of death, to endure misery among men? Tukā says, Let every one learn that I am thy servant.

2876

WHY should I attain liberation as long as I have life? I should lose the comfort of love. Nārāyana is a slave of the Vaishnāvas; what would it profit them to be absorbed into him? What have I lost from my own purse, that I should sit down sunk in silence. For us this pure delight was brought into existence; a luckless mortal is he who repels it. Tukā says, I do not desire absolute union; I will stay in the company of the saints.

2877

THE immortals in heaven petition God, 'Let us be born in the world of mortal men. The name of Nārāyana will liberate our souls; we shall sing songs of praise to the Infinite.' The denizens of Vaikuṇṭha are for ever asking 'When will the servants of Hari come to visit us?' Yama stands ever erect waiting for him with folded hands. Tukā says, To reach the further shore his pious worshippers treasure up the spell of his name.

V.—The all-pervading nature of God

2878

WE have a touch-stone in our own hands,—the truth that God resides in all beings. Yet I seem to have missed the path that the saints travelled by. Tukā says, Pretences are futile; experience alone brings results to pass.

2879

IT is he who sets the mind in motion; in his hands both strings are one. He sets men dancing with various desires, so that they amuse themselves with pleasures. The moon sends so the message to the lotus; iron rises up at the sight the magnet, says Tukā.

2880

THE baby often kicks his mother, yet even that gratifies her. When 'this' and 'that' are united in feeling, then happiness dwells in the mind. Whatever she eats to sustain her life, a portion of it passes on to him. I tell you all freely, says Tukā, the relation is like that of debtor and creditor.

2881

DOES he not dwell in my heart, when he pervades all beings? His grace will guide my spirit, it will set my mind in motion. All my powers are at a standstill; I have carried out no purpose of my own. Tukā says, The post and strings are in his hands; the puppets dance as he sets them dancing.

2882

IF any one thinks that God is in holy-places and others are void of him, this is the error of a man who professes knowledge. God has a good reason for avoiding him; the influence of his past is an obstacle between him and God. The notion that some places are pure and others impure leads to a distinction between things innocent and things sinful; this will bring the wrong consequences. Tukā says, The true secret is that God fills the universe; if we miss this, all religious observances are futile.

2883

O GOD, I will give your secrets into the charge of men, assigning one to each of them; I will guard them myself when the time comes. You need not expand yourself throughout space, since you possess the heart of each man everywhere. An affair that comes in due course of business is easily adjusted, there is no need for violence. Tukā says, To gain a decision I cut myself off from the world.

2884

THE sinful man knows not that one life is like another; he sits down to cut another's throat. God is present as the soul in all created beings; how is it he does not recognize him in the brutes? He sees a soul groaning and howling; yet how do his cruel hands conduct themselves? The villain will go down to hell, says Tukā.

2885

GOD clings to my person, he will not let me go— what am I to do with him? All other gods come and go, but this god keeps with one all through life. His inspiration fills all my limbs; the whole world seems to me to be God. This spirit will not speak out clearly; whatever I do he will not leave me. This deity has devoured my life, with all the five elements of my body. Tukā says, With passionate longing he stands before Pundalika.

2886

WHILE God is all the time in his body, the ill-starred wretch goes wandering idly in search of him. While God is all the time within him, he goes idly from one sacred place to another. The musk is in the naval of the musk-deer, but the deer goes idly wandering about the forest. As the sugar-cane is the very source of sugar, so does God show himself in all creatures. Butter is concealed in milk, but there are men who know not how to churn it out. Tukā says to foolish mankind, How is it you cannot see God in your own bodies?

VI.—The Universality of God's Grace

2887

TUKĀ says, He is impatient in the extreme; it is more than enough that you have met him.

2888

MARK what various creatures were saved by God full easily. Listen to the treasure of his wondrous deeds, for creatures ignorant but devout. A Bhil was taken to Kailasa, who hid himself in the leaves of a tree; a vulture was saved, because it fanned him with its wings. A thief placed his foot on a *pinda*, God took pleasure in that act of worship. Simple and tender of heart, says Tukā, is our master.

2889

THY name was given to a bird, and thus Ganika was saved; a procuress committed unnumbered sins, but when she uttered thy name thou didst take pity on her.

2890

HE will not suffer his care of us to dwindle; his dignity he will maintain. Tukā says, He is the same within and without; he embraces all that embrace him.

2891

THE birds have no store of grain, yet Nārāyana takes thought for them. The python lives in an ant-hill, yet Nārāyana looks after him. The *chātaka* drinks no water from the earth, yet the purple clouds rain for him. We men are but ants, says Tukā, yet do thou fulfil our desires!

VII.—The power of God's name

2892

GANIKA was an adulteress and a whore, nevertheless she was devoted to Raghobā. Sinful as she was, she was carried away in a vehicle from heaven and given a place in eternity. That thou art the Saviour of the Sinful is deeply printed on the three worlds.

2893

THE demon Shanka carried off the Vedas of Bramha, therefore didst thou assume the form of a fish. Did he not throw himself into a trance, and thereby learn what had become of them? Still he called upon thee with joyful devotion; Nārāyana showed himself a sea of mercy. Says Tukā, O Viṭṭhobā I lay hold of thy name; O come to visit me and protect me!

2894

WHY dost thou debar thyself from the might of his name? Why dost thou forget these famous tales? The swords hacked and hewed the body of Pralhāda, but they made not the least impression on it. He called on Rāma, Kṛishṇa and Hari, and the burly demons trembled. Let the power of these glorious deeds live on; Tukā's longing is, O visit me!

2895

A VESSEL of poison was given to Pralhāda, yet thy strength set him free from fear. He drank it down, but it passed on to Nārāyana; his life was saved through thy valiant might. When he contemplated thy name, the poison turned to water in the presence of all. Tukā says, Such are thy glorious deeds; the chief of snakes was wearied in reciting them.

2896

PRALHĀDA was thrown into the fire, but he forgot not Govinḍa. He said to his father,

'All-pervading Hari, Murāri, dwells everywhere.' The fire grew cool, says Tukā; such Vitho, is thy valiant might.

2897

THE stomach in fever can digest nothing but an extract of herbs; when the senses are clouded, men are put in mind of Nārāyana. This name alone will banish at once the fever of the world; beyond doubt it will sweep away all the senses. With other remedies a strict diet is prescribed; there is a sharp and sudden pain, but the cure is a matter of luck. Tukā says, I have opened out the whole matter; good fortune now stands waiting at your door.

2898

THIS name of Viṭṭhala will bring to light things secret and make things invisible manifest. It will teach us to utter the unutterable, it will bring before us the unattainable. If we call out his name without ceasing, we shall receive in abundance things beyond our reach. Tukā says, Those very souls that cling passionately to the world shall be saved by Viṭṭhala's name.

2899

THOUGH a man sin without ceasing, how will it harm him if Viṭṭhala's name dwells with him? As it is when fire catches a heap of grass, so his sins will burn up in a moment. When we look on the feet of Vishṇu's image, how can the actions of our past continue? Tukā says, Where the loud voice of Hari's praise is heard, his name burns up mountains of sin.

2900

EVEN men defiled by countless sins, men unclean to the backbone, even such are purified by Hari's name ere a moment can pass. A man fettered by foul lust, polluted by passion for a *chandāla*, he was taken to Vaikuṇṭha the instant he uttered Hari's name. The root of countless sins came with power over Vālmīka; by Hari's name he was made as pure as Ganges' water. Lead not a life without Hari; it is fair as an image in a mirror; this is why Tukā seeks shelter at Hari's feet.

2901

IF a man utters the name of Viṭṭhobā continually, even sinful men are saved at the sight of him; he breaks the teeth of time.

2902

MAKE haste now to bethink you what is essential and what inessential. By fixing our thoughts on him we have crossed the stream of life wherein is no food. A man born of mortal family, if he remembers to utter 'Rāma', he makes it a rule to repeat it day and night. Tukā says, The millions of his families will be purified.

2903

DAY and night are alike a season of war with us; within, without; war in the world, war in the mind. Day and night unseen powers attack us; they are always advancing and always assaulting us. Tukā says, In the might of thy name we have blackened the faces of all of them.

2904

THY name is like nectar; what need we lack that comes within its range? If we imprison it within our throats we have a cow of wishes there. What mother cannot recognize her own baby? When she hears it cry, her milk streams forth. A man who was never seen to beg feels ashamed when he takes a gift. To preserve their good name men have died on battle-fields; the hero will not turn back from the combat. Tukā says, While we sing him in songs we know him best; what desire have we to see Viṭṭhobā in person.

VIII.—God's generosity and condescension

2905

HE who dwells beyond the six scriptures, Shri Hari, the Self Supreme, he plays in the house of Dasaratha, as Rāma. The peculiar object of Shiva's contemplation, the secret of Vālmīki, Shri Rāma, he eats the Bhil woman's fruit. He who dwells beyond the Yogis' contemplation, he whispers in the monkeys' ears. He who tarries not a moment for the salutations of the chief of beings, he exchanges salutations with monkeys and bears. Tukā bows at the feet of Rāma, the dark-hued, the embodied, the lotus-eyed.

2906

THE book of omens gives you at once what you desire, in the form of a response, but Viṭṭhala gives you immediately either milk or water.

What fruit is possible without good fortune, so long as the mind is full of filth? Tukā says, If your store of merit is small, it will keep you miserable.

2907

GREAT and endued with all attributes as he is, he points out to us the road to Vaikuṇṭha. There is no pride in him; for his worshippers' sake he sits not down. There is neither sloth nor sleep in him, says Tukā; whenever you come he bestows his favour on you.

2908

I AM his servant who is free from all desire, free alike from pleasure and pain. He stands upright on the bank of the Bhima, with his hands upon his hips. What wonder is it that he comes when you call on him; he runs to his worshipper even when he does not remember him. Tukā says, To him will I lift up my song.

2909

HOW he runs like a famished man to wait closely on Pundalika! Nārāyana has forgotten his own dignity! He stands with his hands on his hips; he does not even ask leave to sit down. Tukā says, O Lord of the world, thou dost long for devoted worshippers.

2910

THE sight of him ravishes the mind; Tukā says, To serve his worshippers he runs full speedily, full of shame.

2911

HE serves men and endures harsh words; he bears in mind what is good for them. Tukā says, I play such games as I delight in.

2912

THE magic gem has mines of jewels within it; come, enrich yourselves while this convenient season lasts. There is here no need for debate; the truth or falsehood of this matter has been decided. A platter that has been used you may quietly lay aside; your host knows what your intention is. Tukā says, This is no water doled out in time of scarcity; the fountain will supply as much as you wish.

2913

PARENTS tȧke care of their children and cherish them in the hope of gain. The king of gods is not like them; he is compassionate in his own nature. A mother beats her child when he displeases her; how many fathers beat them, says Tukā, I cannot tell!

2914

VERY merciful art thou, O Lord of the world; O Friend omnipotent in the three worlds!

2915

WHO asks a mother to love her child? It is her infant that creates love in her. It is the yearning of her heart that makes her protect him. O thou that art dark as a cloud, we compare thee to mortal parents, but we see that it adds no grace to thee. The mother guards her child here on earth, but in the next world she is not near him; not so is it with thee. O Infinite One, thou art master of Time! Tukā says, O Nārāyana, thy compassion is greater than hers.

2916

TUKĀ says, Do even apes leave their young behind them at home?

2917

IF a man once follows God, he suffers him not to retrace his steps. God dwells within him, witnessing all his deeds, in a form appropriate to his faith.

2918

GOD assumes many disguises; the best of all his names is Pānduranga. To the cowherd's house he puts forward the name of Murāri. Blest in her good fortune is Yasodā; Govinḍa dances in her courtyard. He turns himself into a slave of his slaves, so Tukā says to Viṭṭhala.

2919

IT is reported in all the world that a temple was turned round, that the milk in Namdeva's hand was drunk up. A cheque drawn by Narsi Mehta was cashed; the fields of Dhanjijat were sown. To save Mirabai, a cup of poison was drained; he turned himself into a Mahāra messenger for Damoji. He assisted at Kabira's loom in weaving lace; a potter's child he brought to life. Show *me* now thy mercy, says Tukā, O king of Pāndhari!

2920

THE offspring of a frog cried out Rāma, Rāma; he suffered not the water to grow hot. A child was writhing in the boiling water; Govind came full speedily to him. He laid his command on the fire: 'thou shalt not burn up these young creatures'. Tukā says, We rejoice to tell these choice tales of his glory.

2921

THE burden of our worldly cares you carry and you enable us to carry; O Infinite One, we have none but thee! In the Gita, with beat of drums, the word is proclaimed that God undertakes to acquire and preserve for his worshippers. He, the four-handed, adorns Arjuna's horses, and acts as his charioteer. Through love of devotion he assumed the part of an eater of corpses; he made Tukā a fixed star in the firmament.

IX.—God's Protecting Love

2922

TUKĀ says, What recompense can the child make? How much indeed does he understand?

2923

WORSHIP consists in loving intimacy; all other views are mistaken. These paradoxical secrets, through error, we cannot comprehend. No price is needed to pacify him; he appreciates loving words. Tukā says, Love must twine our souls and his like threads together.

2924

HOWEVER badly a child speaks, his mother loves to hear him; it is sweet to her because of the love she bears her child, and for the same reason she satisfies his childish longings. He nestles in her bosom, and she bears willingly the thrusts he gives her. Tukā prays to Pānduranga; his case is like the child's.

2925

IN love for his son the father puts by a store, though he famishes himself to that end. He puts a burden on his own arms and shoulders, and soon he makes his son master of an estate. He gladdens his eyes by putting ornaments on him, and he displays the greatness of the store he has made. Tukā says, He will not let any one else vex him, he will risk his own life for him.

2926

HE who implores has no capital but his own entreaties; it rests with him who gives to preserve his own good name. The child runs and lies on his mother's lap to be suckled; it is then for his mother, of her kindness, to give him the breast. Tukā says, Protect us as the tortoise protects its young; the threads of the puppets are in thy hand.

2927

GIVE me my own; I seek nothing new. Assuming his form of a thousand names, this exalted being champions his worshippers. If I speak what cannot be proved, let me be chastised. Tukā says, My real treasure is Viṭṭhala.

2928

THEY are a boat to carry across the sea of the world those of great, those of small authority. Let us tell the story of his deeds in Gokula. Tukā says, Delight in him, for he shows mercy to men.

2929

A MOTHER'S steps are guided by her children's tricks; her love makes her save them from harm at the risk of her life. So powerful over thee is thy love for the saints; to thee I make my entreaty. Thy mind is enchanted by love for men; it is never for a moment forgetful of it. Tukā says, A stream of love pours forth from thy breast.

2930

THE yearnings of love are something that comes from the heart; there is nothing like them. A mother will not let her child cry much; when he is fretful, she is not slow to move. When her face breaks into smiles, the child understands it. Tukā, with all his ignorance, possesses this knowledge; he is not like the run of men.

2931

TUKĀ says, When he hears piteous cries, Viṭṭhala will not show himself slow.

2932

A CHILD may be unkind to his mother, yet still she loves him. She forgets that she is weary; she lifts him on her hip and lays his body against hers. She weeps at his distress; she is ready to give away her life for him. She jumps up when he calls her name, she flings away her life, says Tukā.

2933

WHAT is there that God loves more than worshippers? Nothing else in the three worlds. He loves not Vaikuṇṭha nor the sea of milk; he seizes and stays in his worshippers' minds. With all his heart he finds them altogether sweet; he accepts from them a *tulsi*-leaf with fond delight. He says he has been sold to them altogether; he attends to everything they say. Tukā says, He is a slave to the bliss of devotion; there is nothing else that constrains him.

2934

PARENTS will not injure their own child or see it injured in their presence. The father knows the secret of doing good to his child.

2935

SHE is a boat for the weary, a shade for the worn, she feeds the hungry with the milk of her love. She casts a kindly glance on all; eagerly she waits for them to embrace her. Tukā says, How can there be left us any longer the weariness of pain of unnumbered lives?

2936

If a widow has but an only son, her thoughts are with him day and night. Thou likewise art all in all to me, forsake me not, O Viṭṭhala! All his father's purposes are centered in his beloved son; a chaste wife thinks of nothing but her husband, says Tukā.

X.—God's dependence on his worshippers

2937

At thy own pleasure thou hast taken various names; them I contemplate because of the love I bear thee. God has grown mad, yes mad in his eager desire for worship. He who is above all longing longs; he stretches out his hand for a leaf of *tulsi*. When once he grasps it, says Tukā, he makes no resistance; the key to all is in his feet.

2938

That we fell into sin is thy good fortune; we have bestowed name and form on thee. Had it not been we, who would have asked after thee, when thou wast lonely and unembodied? It is the darkness that makes the light shine; the setting that gives lustre to the gem. Disease brought to light Dhanvantari; why should a healthy man wish to know him? It is poison that confers its value on nectar; gold and brass are high or lowly compared with each other. Tukā says, Know this, O God, that because we exist Godhead has been conferred on you.

2939

WHATEVER be the store of my merit, I will offer it you for a meal; how can you refuse to feed on it? If you stay far from me, who can save me from the whirl of error? Tukā says, Now I possess a power based on love; I shall make the Infinite One do as I have said.

2940

THY thoughts are directed to me, my hunger and thirst are lodged in thee. My tongue delights in one theme; what else am I to speak of? With eager interest in me you stand looking for sweetmeats. Tukā says, Truly what store from the past can exist now?

2941

DOST thou lay the blame on us? It is not right for thee to do so. Tell us this—why didst thou give birth to us? Did it not all depend on thee? Why dost thou keep us at a distance—with this result, that thy own dignity is lowered? Tukā says, Thou shouldst ponder over these questions.

2942

COME, lay thyself prostrate, O Nārāyana, to gain a blessing on thyself. When a son is seated on the throne and rules the country, his father lays his commands on his own head. Tukā says, Position claims respect; why then dost thou hesitate now?

2943

NĀRADA goes ever wandering about the three worlds; Govinḍa wanders with him. Nārada chants sweet hymns; Govinḍa goes with him along the road.

XI.—God acts in us and through us

2944

IF we love truly, there is nothing left but love; we attain to what we pine after. By pulling the string of love he leaves nothing of ourselves in us. Tukā says, Good is contemplation; it is true to the true-hearted.

2945

FAITH in God is God; I have therefore confirmed my trust in him. It is he who gives utterance to my voice, for it is he who sustains the world. I have put together letters, but it is not my own intellect that suggests them. I have not toiled to win the honour or deference of men. A few fortunate people there are who will understand this properly. It is a spring, says Tukā, which has a true source within it.

2946

COUNTLESS fancies rise within my mind; I think of forsaking thy feet. Who is it but you that sets our minds in motion? Tell me even one, O Nārāyana. Tukā says, You have begun to play with me; but when I cease to enjoy the game, what will you do?

2947

THIS is why he has bestowed on men gifts good and bad, that each may have something appropriate to him; such is the marvel accomplished by God. How great is his power! He is both the string and the hand that pulls it. Tukā says, Our eyes are filled with smoke, but truth is truth.

2948

WHOSE controlling power is it that sets our body in motion? Who sets us speaking but Hari? Nārāyana alone puts the world before us and makes us see it; fail not to adore him. It is God who creates in the mind the self-centered view that it alone acts. It is God's power that shakes the leaves of the trees; where, then, is there room for the self-centered view? Tukā says, Vitho pervades the world within and without; what is there that he possesses not in the animate and inanimate worlds?

2949

SUCH faith I have offered thee unreservedly; thou art all to me with all my heart. Knowest thou not all that passes in the heart? Yet thou makest me speak because thou likest to hear me. On thee is placed all my load to bear; in this matter what are words of mine worth? Man's own nature makes him seek his interest through self-interest; thou in thy wondrous doing dost choose this impulse for thy own purpose. Thou knowest well, O God, says Tukā, our innermost nature.

V

The Problem of Action

I.—The perplexing aspect of the world

2950

THOU dost create for thy amusement; this is all a diversion of thine. Yet between us, mankind and thee, thou hast interposed the sense of self. Hence evil spirits may enter this world, and show or hide themselves at will. How long, says Tukā, will thou torment us?

2951

YOU cannot bring into harmony the views that God is one with us, and that he is other; so remember Nārāyana! This alone can make all things perfect—union with the Unchanging, the uttering of his name; delight in him. The eddies of sense come surging like robbers along every path; they sweep along even such as have reached the threshold of safety. Tukā says, Nothing but this faith can carry you through; this is the whole secret.

2952

THOU has set anger and lust to pursue me; I have been sorely troubled by them, O God! These belong to thee, O God; I am greatly amazed that thou canst not control them. They may amuse thee, but they cost us our souls; we are always full of grief and fear. Tukā says, This is the effect of our own destiny; who would ridicule thee, the All-Powerful One?

2953

WITH such snares thou hast entangled us—as thou shouldst not have done, O God! This flood has come upon us from afar and swept us along with it. We do not understand what is happening; thou shouldst not shut thine eyes. Tukā says, Let us embrace each other.

2954

WHAT a love of the world thou hast implanted in us! Thou hast given it us for a possession. Thou art cruel, O God! Thou wilt not make us say 'Enough of desire!' Thou seest us caught in the chain of actions, but thou standest apart and wilt not cut it short. Tukā says, In calling thee mine I feel I have taken a burden upon me in vain.

2955

THE body is carried on by the course of its past; this is deeply grievous to us. Run to me, O Nārāyana, and wake me up! Tukā says, Whence do these experiences overtake us? They have no real existence; they are a disease of ourselves.

2956

IT is thou who settest in motion the activities of our mind, who hast made us fit for the business of life. Yet, whatever happens, thou dost not take the burden of it on thyself; and whom, pray, am I to call greater than thou? The five elements are like empty bags of leather; what faith in them is either warranted or unwarranted? Tukā says, There is no need for discussion here; why should we vex ourselves to no purpose?

2957

O NĀRĀYANA, if thou dost not come to set me free, I cannot escape from the power of Time. These words may set me free; what other resource have I? I have not yet filled up the measure of actions done; the obstacles in my path will ruin me. Tukā says, My soul is full of dread; run swiftly in response to my prayers.

2958

WHY dost thou not show thy mercy towards me, that my mind may find peace in the centre of all things? Then neither good nor evil would enter it; it would attain the welcome consummation of peace. I am oppressed by the mutations of the five elements; the generous one should protect me from these by making me insensible to the world. Break the neck of my sense of self, says Tukā.

II.—The impossibility of escaping our past

2959

IT is not thy generosity that is to blame; we do not show thee whole-hearted faith. What canst thou do, O God, with our *karma*? It is impossible to deal with it, says Tukā.

2960

LOOK, O God, what mankind are like, each differing according to his store of merit. No one resembles another; men show themselves pure or base. In each, the five elements form a single heap; how the threads set them dancing! Tukā says, Each finds himself in a position corresponding to his nature.

2961

WHAT it is your purpose to do, will it not be done? O listen to my stammering speech! The power that suffers me not to live—if it kills me, I may die; yet there is still left the store of my actions. Tukā says, All remedies have failed, therefore I have remembered thy feet.

2962

THE fields are flooded with water when the time comes; there is no use in following any other course. This is ordained by the Doer of all; the measure is filled to the brim with rules for everything. Should the clouds pour down rain in the cold or the hot weather, the rain poured out will be waste of effort. Tukā says, Some grubs live in poison and others in nectar; if you change their habitations they will not live.

2963

EVERYTHING is in the power of fate working through our past; I must crave the pity of fate. My mind has inspired me with this view;

and as long as I hold it, I shall acknowledge no other God than luck. When we have done with the grumbling complaints of the world, you will come to seat yourself where the power of faith calls you. Tukā says, We should set you there and worship you; we should attribute no other powers to you.

2964

MY parents are full of mercy, but my own designs have severed me from them. This was not because my store of merit led me astray; destiny unseen has been my close companion. I am chafing now at my ignorance of thy secret, though I know well the rules of religion. Tukā says, He stands erect, he will not sit down; he is indeed our mother, and he is alarmed about us.

2965

I NEED not fear any one; but you, O ye people, are oppressed with dread. Tukā says, In whatever form the fruit of our past overtakes us, we must accept it.

2966

GOOD men do not discard their friends; but God has taken this view of others. Be it so; what force can prevail against him now? Our own destiny is brought on us. Who can argue against a man in high power? Each must put up with his own life. Tukā says, I make no complaint against you, O God; I have not served you with my whole mind.

III.—Nothing is gained by the works of the law or by austerities

2967

WE must first clear the road, then we can walk along it without getting caught in anything. This principle of the wise and good has come down from ancient times; a traffic in guilt and merit is full of snares. If you have to run, throw aside your cloak; if you are encumbered you will be caught. Tukā says, This is how to distinguish the valiant; weak creatures are caught in the snares of time.

2968

THOUGH I made myself ceremonially purè, some impurity would cling to me; my rules about taking or leaving, about words to be uttered, would be principles merely which I should not practise. So, at one step, I have surrendered my body to thee; now keep me at thy feet. In every ceremony errors arise, a fruitful cause of sin; the rope I make is the source of death. Tukā says, It is thou who settest in motion the universe; why should I feel any anxiety about it?

2969

I AM well-off now where I am; the generous one has put me in my right place. If we take on to our head the load of words, it grows heavier, and we cannot lift it off. I shall accustom my mind to silence; I shall not let qualities develop themselves in me. Tukā says, We shall live with the cowherds; I know well what keeps me safe.

IV.—Our faith a reward of merit

2970

TELL me now faithfully what I should do, O God! ceremonial rites avail not to free us from our *karma*; they end in nothing but trouble undergone. Tukā says, Do not try me to the last; give the gift of thy grace to him who begs for it.

2971

WHY do you ascribe so many reasons for this? It is the ripening of my own store of merit. Viṭṭhala has rubbed the film of darkness from my eyes, so that I see the world full of the joy of Bramha. Tukā says, I have become a stranger to desire; my delight dwells in Govinḍa.

2972

THE seed assures us of fruit if we take care of it and water it. If you take a bite at it through greedy desire, the misadventure will end in a piteous cry. This body of ours is but a narrow strip of land; such sentiments ripen there as you sow; if you narrow your soul, you will compass nothing but lamentations. If a man buries his wealth underground, and leads a life of wretched penury, though happiness is next-door to him, his delusion makes him wretched. Tukā says, If a man loses his bearings, he wanders away from the place he wants to go to; what I say in this matter is final, it is proven by experience.

2973

YOU are wasting this precious life, which your store of merit bestowed on you. After waiting for the end of countless rebirths, a human body you have received; if you employ it to profit yourself, you will serve your true interest. Fix your thoughts then on Viṭṭhala, to ensure your happiness. As men lay up a store of hoarded treasure, so do you store up Nārāyana. Practise devotion to Hari; it will much avail you in the next world, it will save you from Yama. Tukā says, Set a value on your life; spend not your voice save in uttering God's name.

2974

MOONLIGHT to thieves, a virtuous neighbourhood to whores, potsherds to the magic stone, all these are useless. You may throw stones into boiling milk, but they will never grow soft. Tukā says, If a man is duly prepared by past merits, then only will his mind be willing to stay with the saints.

2975

WHEN by chance the dust from the saints' feet touches us, the seed of desire is burned up within us. There is born in us then a delight in the name of Rāma; our throat is choked by love, tears stream from our eyes; the form of Rāma shows itself in the heart. Tukā says, This means of attainment is easy to grasp and very sweet, but it is only revealed to the fully-meritorious.

2976

FOR our sins in the past our body is punished; no blame rests on thee, O Nārāyana! A man sows bitter cummin seeds and looks for fruits of nectar; but how can plantains grow on the swallow-wort? Pleasure and pain are the appointed lot of the body; a man should not throw away knowledge. Tukā says, A man should not grow angry with God; he should ask his own mind 'What have I done?'

2977

AS is the store of our past, such are the thoughts that rise in our minds; what we preach to a man produces no effect on him. The treasure that each has laid up comes running to meet him; there is no need to counsel him. Though a man hears counsel, his own qualities come to light; his destiny proves what they are, says Tukā.

2978

THE wife of a young husband and the wife of an old one were bosom friends; they were talking over their lives together. 'My husband is very, very small; he goes and plays with other boys.' 'Listen to my troubles, dear; my husband is an old man who goes about coughing.' 'He stays out-of-doors and plays till evening; I lie in bed waiting for him.' 'There is something wrong with my past; how can I tell you my miseries? When I approach him to embrace him, he won't let me come near him; he grows cross.' This is all the treasure of our past, says Tukā; how can we blame God?

V.—Rebirth, its cause and how to escape it

2979

HOW many times am I to be born, to be always an object of scorn? I have a load of actions on my back, it will not let me step forward. Tukā says, Here is this scorn ready waiting for me.

2980

HE who follows this path lives for ever; he escapes from the world. The servants of Vishṇu see no more rebirth. His power is over the three worlds, he is now the saviour of poor Tukā.

2981

LEAVING this portion of happiness, the fool begs for liberation. Why should we not accept mortal birth, and plunder the love that resides in his name? Here we have curds and rice given us; there is no talk of this in Vaikuṇṭha. Tukā says, I desire not absolute union with God.

2982

IF you delay your progress on the path, where can you make up your loss afterwards? If the impressive shows of the world arrest you, then the pangs of rebirth will overtake you. Tukā says, If jewels are alloyed with base metal, only the fire can make them true gold again.

2983

THIS secret I missed, hence I was caught in the chain of action. It pursues me closely and destroys me; it makes me pass through the womb. Because we imagine 'Mine' and 'Thine' to be different, the tether of illusion is fastened about our necks. Tukā says, I am made a beast of burden; I am frightened by tracks that have no reality about them.

2984

MEN will never know how to drink a sweet juice like this of Nārāyana. It heals the disease of life, so that the pain thereof comes back no more. No struggle is needed; the disease simply cannot dwell within your frame. A change very swiftly passes over us; we are absorbed into God. The pain of birth and death ebbs away; the snare of the world is rent open. Tukā says, This draught has shown its power in many cases.

2985

THERE was a string of pots tied each by the neck to the revolving wheel; then one vessel was broken, and I became free from toil and emancipated. The broken potsherd cannot keep its place, or perform its exacted toil, or go round in the circuit. Tukā says, How can the corpse feel any joy or interest in the fire?

2986

I AM content if this life is wasted, and I return to birth again, since I stand before thee as thy servant, in no hurry, free from fear. Whether I have too little or enough, I leave the burden of this care to Pānduranga. O mother Viṭṭhala, why need I look after myself? Wherever I go, in accordance with my lot, I shall not forget thee, O Cowherd! By one stroke I have secured my own welfare; know now thy own O Nārāyaṇa, says Tukā.

2987

HE is the begetter of my soul, the begetter in gross of all souls. In Janārdana, the chain of men's actions is brought to a close; but with other gods, the mischief of error still goes on. If we fail to keep our minds awake, we may confound left with right. Tukā says, If you cut branches and leaves from a tree, though you sprinkle them with water, they will soon be dead.

2988

THE more I crave for objects of sense, the longer sojourn in the womb is my portion, the more there clings to me the sin of desiring the unreal. Now, be things as they will, let repentance dwell in me; only let me get rid of 'Mine' and 'Other's' As long as we are awake, what can a dream destroy? When the words of men annoy us, we should look on the pain they cause us as unreal. An ape is irritated by his image in a well; he jumps in there, but what does he find? Tukā says, He breaks his head and knees and elbows.

2989

WHEN shall I see the day that will bring a blessing on lucky and luckless men alike?

In the last hour of life we may embrace his feet, when we part hastily from our bodies. Let us be done with this chain of actions, this tangle we have woven round ourselves; my mind has grown impatient, O God! At every step I take, I remember that countless disorders arise within us; so my soul trembles, and I cry vehemently to thee. Thou must have heard my cry, says Tukā; why dost thou try me to the last?

2990

IF they miss the way, he makes them find it straight in front of them; thus Hari's servants know not what it is to sojourn in the womb. What do we know of past actions clinging to us? They are destroyed. Tukā says, I will open my eyes wide, I will feel no pangs.

2991

O MIND of mine, bury thyself in God's feet; do not stray abroad as the senses impel thee! All happiness is centered there; time and the cycle of time cannot end it. The going, coming, and running of rebirth will cease; we shall have no mountains to cross. I have this only to tell thee, Look on wealth and women as though they were poison. Tukā says, We shall be grateful to you if we cross the stream of the world.

2992

MANY a soul was comforted by thee in earlier days; thou art the mother of the helpless.

Whomsoever thou receivest, he enters the world no more. There is none so powerful as thou; none that, like thee, pervades the world. To thee therefore I have surrendered my soul completely. I have thrown my body into a trance and made it useless.

2993

SIT still with devoted faith, and let not the world entangle your thoughts. Settle firmly the king of Pandhari in your heart; then further steps will present themselves to you. Offer no worship to any God; no counting of beads, no penance, no meditation. If you consider anything your own, observe, you will not fail to be reborn. How many times have you entered a body already? Why do you not recognize your opportunity now? Wake up and seize it, and learn what this joy is like. What you can gain there is a secret easily learned; weigh it in the scales in the light of your own experience. Wake up, says Tukā, and in this one life break off from you the fetters of the world.

2994

THIS body became mine by pure accident; what no means could accomplish has come to pass. Now cut short my course of rebirth, give me freedom from fear. A blind man may hit on a treasure-trove behind his back, against all probability; just so, this has come to pass. Tukā says, It was a welcome chance; now, O God, I shall quit thy side no more.

2995

LET there dwell in my mind love and the assurance, that in sleeping, waking, and dreaming I am one with Viṭṭhala. I ask for nothing else, neither royal power nor wealth. Bestow thy love upon me so that I may see thee everywhere; let the experience of my mind never be shut up within itself. Cut down at the root the evil done by us in birth and death. My body undergoes a change at the sight of thee; it is crammed with the principle of all life; individuality is crushed, I am saved by meditating on thee. Possessing this faith, says Tukā, we find thy name sufficient for us. Birth after birth is welcome to overtake us, whatever station it place us in.

2996

THIS is a good old deity, simple and trustful, such as his worshippers have made him by their faith; so we his worshippers fear not to pass through the womb and enter the world. Tukā says, We have secured the company of God, and we never neglect one another.

2997

THE musk-melon when ripe loses its bitterness; so has Pānduranga done with us. Lust and wrath have subsided into their own places; the whole world is full of joy. Memory and forgetfulness, faith and doubt are all gone; we have become Pānduranga himself. Tukā says, *Good Fortune* is what we must call this; for the sake of this we ought to accept rebirth.

2998

OUR seed of life is like a parched and puffed-up grain; we have no birth or death before us. What room is there for concrete shape in us? Our body is turned manifestly into God. The sugar-cane springs not from dry sugar; how can *we* pass into the womb again? Tukā says, We have conquered all our appetites; we see Pāndu-ranga in all vessels.

2999

AS a loving wife holds her husband dear; as a blue-jay longs for the moon; with such a love, if I embrace the feet of Viṭṭhala, I need never pass through the womb again. As a famine-stricken man delights in a meal, or a thirsty man in water, or a lover in his paramour, with such a passion, says Tukā, should you seek Pāndurang; he will carry you to the further shore.

3000

THE senses will profit you nothing; make haste to utter with your tongue Rāma's name. Good health is not your own possession; it is idle, it is futile, it is a shadow of the illusive world. Tukā says, The essence of our life is the utterance of Hari's name; apart from Hari, there is nothing but birth and rebirth.

3001

TWENTY lakhs of rebirths you must pass in plants; nine lakhs in creatures of the water; eleven lakhs in insects; ten lakhs in birds; thirty lakhs in beasts; four lakhs in human form; a crore of times you return to each womb, then the wind of manhood will blow upon you. Only then, says Tukā, does man attain a man's body; he is a fool if he wastes it.

VI.—The sense of sin

3002

I AM caught and imprisoned by the five elements; I am fast bound by the sense of self. I have tied my own neck, not knowing all the time that I was free. Why did I imagine this world was real? Why did I look on 'Mine' as true? I lusted after a small portion of pleasure; in the end, I brought destruction on myself. Let me now sacrifice my body, says Tukā; let me burn up the store of my past.

3003

A WORN-OUT ox is belaboured because it will not rise from the spot when it lies down. Even so obstinate is my mind; run to me; I abhor this spirit of self-will! If a man leaps down a precipice in fear of a pursuer, he knows not whether he will live or die. Tukā says, Such an affliction as this do I suffer; I call upon Pānduranga.

3004

I AM not truly thy servant, though I call myself such; this is merely a shift contrived for some purpose. What duty really requires from *you*, consider for yourself. As for me, my conduct is not pure; but I fix my thoughts on his feet. O Pānduranga, says Tukā, knowest thou not this?

3005

MY eyes are opened; I shall know what happiness is like when thou givest it me; Tukā says, I realize this while my soul is severed from thee, O God.

3006

THE right has been given, but the mind cannot profit by it; the attributes that envelop the mind war against it; lust, anger, arrogance, jealousy, selfishness, fault-finding, dislike, utter folly, and greed. These heavy forces of the senses roam about like thieves, seeking to dig or break into houses. Against them all efforts of mine fail; the secret of success thou alone knowest. Now then, says Tukā, I shall take such steps as will lead me to thy feet.

3007

I HAVE placed my capital in the power of the false, so my business must end in a loss. How then, with what face must I expect to look on thee? I find myself a prisoner in the womb. I am dyed with the hue of objects dug from the four mines, through consorting with good and bad. Vexations from many sources have changed me much; the course of time has deeply dyed me. I can no more undo the folds that envelop me, so as to show what is within. Transform me, therefore, says

Tukā, by placing me near thee; make a little cowherd of me, O God!

3008

ARE those few whom you saved in ancient days, who were lost souls like myself? While I am praising thee, can sin dwell in me? What strength can it still possess? Tukā says, Thou didst make stones float in the sea; I am as heavy as they, O God!

3009

I OBEY your injunctions, nevertheless I am much afraid of you. So I make your feet my familiar friends; I do not ask to sit beside you. With folded hands, I stand waiting before you. Tukā says, O ye Saints, I am a sinful man.

3010

WHAT prayer can I put up? Who will decide that what I say has found favour? O Store of Grace, I can form no inference concerning this. Most piteous cries have I uttered; no answer have I heard. Up till now, I felt sure that some of my service had been accepted. Tukā says, Now nothing but the struggle is left me; I see no sign of assurance in him who stands hand on hip.

3011

MY writings are blackened with shame, for thou givest me no peace of mind. How can I feel joyful when no words are uttered? There is no pleasure in a meeting if no love is expressed at it.

If a man turns his elbow to another when he meets him, it is easy to see there is but a shred of love left them. What powers I had, I have spent; now I have no skill to act or devise. Mighty art thou, O God, says Tukā; how can the service of a weak man reach thee?

3012

I HAVE not risen into notice at thy feet; thou dost not even ask where I am gone. Why should I lead a life of worldly cares? Hitherto I have been a burden on the earth. Tukā says, O Lord of Pandharī, the disease of life is an overpowering torment.

3013

WHAT has brought about this distance between us? Tukā says, Some suggestion of a cause has crossed my mind.

3014

I AM ruined by sloth; I am sorely oppressed by desire. They have stolen from my mouth the utterance of thy name; whereas once I was near, I am now far removed from thee. How was it that I fell into this dual conception, that drags me farther and farther from thee? Tukā says, Now let God take me to himself and set me free.

3015

ALL the past will be forgotten, the restless grief we suffered. In this critical hour, unite us to each other; our minds will find repose at thy feet I have made myself worthless by serving the body; thus I can see no truth in thee. Tukā says, Show thy generosity; I am ready, with full attention, to receive thy gift.

3016

I HAVE ceased to form any views of my own. False assumptions and regard for honour destroy all the plans I had settled. Tukā says, I might be upset in less than a moment; protect me O God!

3017

I KNOW not how to worship or serve thee; I stand before thee constrained by fear. I have lost my bearings; I make a circuit round myself; I am wearied out by error. Tukā says, I observe thy commands; I have set my soul in one spot.

3018

THERE continues not within my heart a single motion towards thee; I remember thee not, but forget thee. What amazement this experience brings with it, I have my own mind to testify to this. Though I admonish my mind, it will not repose; how can I control it from moment to moment? Tukā says, Too many transactions of life I have taken part in; my soul is deeply dyed with their hue.

3019

MY soul is held fast by the oppression of desire, regrets of many kinds are present in my mind. Like a pressed labourer, I see no fruit of my toil; I am stiff and cramped by the cold.

Tukā says, I have no influence at thy feet; my sins are overpowering and keep me from meeting thee.

3020

SUCH is the rule; forget it not, O Pānduranga! Though I kept my mind from wavering, still it is full of fear; it is subject to joy and grief. Tukā says, Your decision will be plain; it was your glorious fame that made me desire to see you.

3021

SUCH is my experience which has been with me all my life. Desire has been close at my back; nothing can still it. I do not know where to go, nor any means to dismiss it. Tukā says, It bears a million pangs within it.

3022

HOW can we reach our aim? Our desires increase our sufferings. What can we do as long as these dwell with us? What we ought to long for is thou, Pānduranga. I have no delight in thy form; I break my heart with desires. Tukā is not carried away by my any outward splendour.

3023

I HAVE crossed over mountains of grief; but I have found my true welfare at your feet alone. We are annoyed by the sight of rotten fruit; we feel the difficulty of a difficult path. I know I am not forsaken, but I feel despondent; the day I am looking forward to does not arrive. Good fortune is with thee, O God, says Tukā; thou art the only refuge for my soul.

3024

THOU wilt help us of thine own free will; why should I entreat thee in this way? My prayer for mercy is still unanswered; my soul is still a soul apart from thee. How can the seed sprout unbidden, without the warmth of parental love? Tukā says, I will mortify my body, if this entreaty will make thee approach me.

3025

WHY have I lived on, a mere burden on the earth? I have found no shelter at thy feet. What use are my eyes to me? 'Twere better that I lost them; they see not the Supreme. What is my mouth but a burrow or den of wild beasts, if it utters not thy name continually? Tukā says, The virtuous soul cannot live for a moment without Pānduranga.

3026

WE have proclaimed to the world that we are thy servants; it will not be right for thee now to forsake us. Who would care to enquire into my merits? Thy name is Purifier of the Sinful. We are fast bound by greed and error, but who, O Infinite One, is responsible for this? Tukā says, Truly I am a sinful man, but I seek shelter in thee.

3027

WHY do sins cross my path, though I have offered thee my sense of self? O Pānduranga, gracious and merciful, thou wilt have power to control all this! Why should any others have power to control us, as long as we are near thee? Tukā says, I have told my tale at thy feet; bestow on me a gift that is fit for me; thou hast the power.

3028

WHAT sort of line has he written on my forehead? There is no escape from this misery.

3029

I HAVE surrendered my body to thee, yet I still entertain fears. Well I know I have made this blunder, that destroys the confidence I felt. Dolt that I am, I experience not within me what I describe. Thou oughtest to punish me well, O Viṭṭhala!

3030

I AM nothing but a heap of all sins; thou art altogether the best of all beings. Even as I am, receive me; thou hast to bear all my burdens. Time has swallowed me up altogether; but thou hast all power within thyself. Tukā says, I have ceased now to take any steps for myself; thy feet are everything to me.

3031

WHAT can I do now to this mind of mine? In spite of all my prayers it will not stand still; it behaves to me courteously, yet it seeks to drag me down to hell. Run to me, O Hari; I can see none likely to restrain it save thou. It will not stand still one moment; it scatters my attention violently. It is full of eddies of sensual pleasure;

it is bent on plunging into the sea of the world. Hopes and projects are full of sin; they have ruined me altogether. Tukā says, O Bearer of the Disc, why dost thou still delay?

3032

ILLUSION has beaten him sorely, yet there is no scar upon his skin; pain of mind, however, sets his hair on end. He can find no opportunity to escape from its power; he cannot speak, he is gagged. No help can reach him; he can find no point of vantage to attack it from; no clue to track it by. In his fear of it, he smears his body with ashes; but it afflicts him with violent disorders. Tukā says, Desire assaults all men in the rear; it will not suffer them to cry to God.

3033

HOW can I win the favour of the saints? How can I remember God's names? This is my anxious thought; when I lie down to sleep I cannot close my eyes. When I take my meals, I find no food sweet or wholesome; I feel the pleasures of the senses a burden.

3034

I AM troubled sorely by fear; the world will terrify me by telling me things I have never heard from the saints. The servants of Vishṇu, they will say, have no path to salvation; all their trouble is in vain. They will scorn me for singing thy praises; how can I express the misery I shall feel? I am cast down, says Tukā; how shall I meet this occasion, O Pāndurangа?

3035

SOMETHING has stolen from us the utterance of his name; we once were near him, now we have drifted away from him. How have we fallen into the power of this view,—that God is other than we? These forces drag us hither and thither. Indolence has stripped my mind naked, my cravings have much tormented me. Tukā says, Be with me now, O God, and keep me safe.

VII.—Reproaches and challenges to God

3036

I PERCEIVE thou hast forgotten me; why should I live longer? What canst thou do with the store of my past? My life is now a curse to me. I heard thy name, thy established fame, as Saviour of the Sinful, therefore I hoped on; now I have found thee pitiless. I have lost all hope, says Tukā; for thy sake I shall destroy myself.

3037

WHEN time justifies it, thou takest thy gift back; as though a donor knew not what lay just in front of him! Tukā says, I am already one destined to die; why dost thou make thyself to blame for it?

3038

THE Purānas are ashamed; the Veda grows feeble; we who hold by thy name look wretched and pitiable. The words of the Saints are wasted. Thus, says Tukā, thy service is openly brought to nought.

3039

MEN set up drinking-places in compassion for the poor; why dost not thou, O Pānduranga, likewise build a boat for us? Men give medicine to the sick, and ease their pain; they leap into the water to save the drowning; they clear thorns off the road for those that follow them; they bear the burdens of the weary, says Tukā.

3040

I AM amazed that any misery should overtake him who has thy name in his mouth. How can I tell? Perchance thou mayest fall asleep; I know not, O Viṭṭhala! It is thou who must break the snares of the world; why hast thou neglected this? I am shocked, says Tukā; it would seem that I have troubled myself in vain.

3041

A SERVANT should do the work appointed him; that the seal on his orders should stand for righteousness, the master must take care. I know not if thou has lost all stoutness of heart; it seems thou hast grown feeble. That might, which should have filled us thy servants with strength, thou seemest at this season to have renounced. Send speedily, says Tukā, a messenger to call me, or tell me what I must do.

3042

O GOD, thou forgettest why we have burned up the world. I know not why thou hast thus cast me down, crushing my love towards thee. I have offered thee my body; art thou not ashamed to count me a pollution? Tukā says, For whose sake have I cast away all desire, and wander about indifferent to the world?

3043

I HAVE placed no demand before thee; yet thou art troubled for fear I should worry thee. Do not think, however, that any device will save thee from my importunities. I cannot bear to be parted from thee now; it would be death to me to quit thy feet. Tukā says, What I ask thee for now is a dwelling-place at thy feet.

3044

WE are sinful, thou art the Purifier; know that this truth is descended from the past. We must not make out the old to be new; let each keep its own province. We must take all needful steps to preserve the spot we have inherited. Tukā cries aloud and compels God to listen.

3045

BE without form to those who would have thee such; we love to see thee in thy own true form. Can a baby be treated like a boy that has grown to knowledge? Can he be kept at a distance? When men are eagerly bent on salvation, thou keepest circling round them elusively; when they are mad after knowledge, thou tantalisest them. Tukā says, Where canst thou find a chance to banish from thee my devotion?

3046

WHEN I behold thee, I shall begin to serve thee; naught else, O God, do I need. As to food and clothes, they depend on my past; but do thou steady my mind and set it at thy feet. My mind is so tortured by the world that I am drawn to thee; I delight in thy name and form. What! Hast thou no capital, that my words must needs be wasted? When the magic stone touches iron and turns it into gold, does it take account of the merits of the iron? Tukā says, Consider not what I am; vindicate thine own name.

3047

KNOW you not what is in my mind? Yet this is your pleasure, O Nārāyana,—that answers to you should ever grow in numbers, that your worshippers should put thee to shame, that they should always be grumbling. When have good words been wasted? A child loves toys, says Tukā.

3048

WHEN will the promptings of my mind be justified? Quite lame am I; canst thou not see this?

3049

ALL my entreaties have been wasted; I am still left full of trouble. What consolation has he given me; what longings of mine has he satisfied? I am sorely dejected, for I have not, even asleep, seen him in a vision; how then can he have spoken out to me directly? Be ashamed henceforth, O Pānduranga, that worshippers abandoned like me have lived in the world. Tukā says, I have no confidence left; I feel that thou hast given me up.

3050

IT is in thy power to make a mountain into a grain of mustard-seed, ere one eyelid can meet the other. Whence then, says Tukā, this delay in saving a poor gnat like me?

3051

I AM sure thou never hadst a baby of thine own; tell me why thou disappointedst me. If thou knewest already that I was a sinner, why didst thou shelter me at thy feet? I am the branded slave of Hari, so no difference should be made between me and others in the row of saints. Tukā says, We have unquestionably won the victory; it is thy part now to make up our shortcomings.

3052

IN whatever station thou shalt cause me to be born, I will never give up thy name. I shall pass on to thee pleasure and pain, as I experience them; then why need I suffer any anxious care? Even though I have to sojourn in the womb, I shall call myself thy branded slave, O Viṭṭhala! Why need I entreat thee to save me? Thou wilt thyself be brought low; for this reason thou wilt save us, says Tukā.

3053

I AM amazed that *thou* art not bold enough; as for me, my soul issues forth from me, crying, Come! Come! Somehow, the whole world seems to me desolate without thee. Why, O Pānduranga, dost thou not listen to me?

3054

NOW I will finish off everything at one meal; I will have done with continual requests. Make my last mouthful sweet, O Pānduranga, mother mine. Practise no sort of deception on us now; thy little ones are grown up. Tukā says, Thou must not tease us now; I shall not leave one dish unfinished.

3055

WHILE we do not comprehend thee, thou mayest very well deceive us; but afterwards, what is the good of turning thy back on us? I have caught thee now, thou must let me have my turn; when thou art found, this mood of faith follows. While I kept my eyes shut, thou wert far from me; now I have caught sight of thee, and I gaze on thee steadily. Tukā says, It is thy habit to say 'No'; but I am no common beggar.

3056

THERE are many led astray by errors; they torment their own bodies. No confidence can be placed in their talk; I gird up my loins to utter thy name. With a single impulse I have steadied my own soul; the responsibility for all is thine. Do not let thy own branded cattle be hurt; do as seems best to thee. Tukā says, How often must I implore thee? Perchance Nārāyana will grow angry.

3057

WE say, there is no one to prevent thee from coming to us; it seems thou art afraid. It must be my own fate that has turned thee back; though thou sustainest the universe, thou hast no power to control fate. We put full trust in thee, we often cry out thy name. Tukā says, The five elements have entrapped me and laid me on the threshing-floor.

3058

WHEN a child's mother is dead, who asks after his welfare? Who cares for orphans? Be assured, this is the common course of things. When good luck meets with good luck, people look on with interest and admiration. Tukā says, As long as we are near God, we are like gods ourselves.

3059

WHAT is left between us now that is fit for me to celebrate? I have hardened my mind, though I have not found peace. We may all waste away at home, even as we waste away with thee. Tukā says, Let us roll up thy divinity and lay it aside.

3060

FIVE times did I call thee, yea seven; why was no message or greeting sent me? I know not why Nārāyana has so hardened his heart; I can hit on nothing that will please him. I cannot tell, says Tukā, whether the fruit that grows within him is sweet or bitter.

3061

WHY was this worldly fame of mine fostered,—why not brought to a definite end? My spirit would have escaped these restless pangs; I should have known their cause. Tukā says, You must make some definite decision; reticence in the physician is death to the patient.

3062

DO promptly now what thou wilt; there is no distance left between us now. If we are each to bestow words and glances on the other, why needest thou call in any witness to prove we have done so? Tukā says, I have complained to thee till I am dying; this is now plain to thee.

3063

I OUGHT not to speak to thee in hard terms; but a child is wont to show too familiar presumption. Thou must pardon any offence that has been given thee; teach us better, O thou who art best of all. A child will run to take hold of a flame; he does not know that he will be burnt; his mother must drag him back from it. Tukā says, The mother who bears the child must pass the after-birth also; this thou knowest well, O God.

3064

IF the child of wealthy parents go about in rags, whom will people laugh at? The rich and powerful feel ashamed for their name's sake; they take thought for those that seek their protection. If thou meanest to do anything that is right, then save this fallen wretch, Tukā.

3065

I COME before thee, with my loins girt up, to urge by force my request. Send me back with the gift of thy love, repaying the debt of thy service. Show thyself wise; let the world know nothing about it. Tukā says, I hold thy feet fast; what else is there for me to do?

3066

I AM no mere slave of desire, that thou shouldst have made me look eagerly for a gift from thee. Thou canst well discern the heart; thou shouldst deal with me fairly. Since thou hast once formed a design, to check it would be sinful; we call this violation of a purpose. Tukā says, I cannot bear to be tormented thus; when food is once cooked, it is waste of labour to keep it boiling on the fire.

3067

IF he is too niggardly to give away buttermilk, is it likely he will spread us a feast? His conduct shows that he means nothing. What expense did I fetter thee with? How have I caused thee any embarrassment? Nothing shall cling to my body but thy service; such is my fixed resolution. Tukā says, To vindicate thy name, take up thy work after my precedent.

3068

WHERE I have fixed my gaze, there my mind is closely bound up. If thou findest this oppressive, banish me from thee; if thy food is polluted it may make thee vomit. I am amazed that thou shouldst find thyself in difficulties over anything of this kind. Tukā says, Raise thy hand at once if thou wilt; I will proclaim thy fame.

3069

WHY is not the goodness of God brought home to us by experience? What delay is there on thy side? What I ask for seems to be near thee; if I set up a quarrel with thee, what shall I gain by it? I shall not abandon the respectful demeanour of a servant; I will follow constantly the course thou hast laid down for me. Tukā says, Thou hast withdrawn thy hand from every pledge; but there is no new purpose in my mind.

3070

SAY, if thou wilt, I am a foolish man, but say *something* O Nārāyana. I have followed this line of conduct to force thee to speak somewhat. Let me but induce thee to assume a visible shape; be angry then if thou wilt. I am fully conscious of what I want; but the time is passing, says Tukā.

3071

WHERE, O God, did I go about to bring pressure on thee, to make thee lose thy true character, and waste thy principal? It is but a poor man that prays to thee, yet thou hast prepared thyself to ruin him. I have heard of no case like this, says Tukā.

3072

IN time to come thou shouldst serve up new dishes to us; one by itself is not tasty enough. When a woman puts on a new ornament, her body is commended; one change should follow another visibly and quickly. When service makes the servant look more handsome, the master's fame is spread in the three worlds. Tukā says, Fill me with joy to-day; I will sound thy praises and dance before thee.

3073

IF I am singly devoted to things of the world, to whom will *they* be devoted? Give this point your consideration. You have materials within yourself to think over; the features of the image reflected resemble those of the original. If the omen is auspicious, its result is auspicious; the experience of the present forecasts the future. Tukā says, So far as I remember you, so far shall I be able to fix my faith on your feet.

3074

SINCE thou hast made my life dependent on others, what fault in me has made thee abandon me? I pray to thee earnestly, yet no room is made for me; it is not right thus to shut me out. Tukā says, Why didst thou originally give birth to so many children? Why dost thou forget this, O Pānduranga?

3075

AS long as I was ignorant, I raised no such cry as this; but now I have found the true path. If the child of a rich man cries out for pity, what sort of treatment will people think he receives? Tukā says, We have loudly proclaimed thy praises; but in the daily course of our lives we are parted from thee.

3076

THIS was no time for thee to shun the distressed. I know not why thou holdest not forth thy hand; how canst thou bear to see me weeping? Thou showest us a hope, and then runnest from us, so that we cannot catch thee. Tukā says, Though we run after thee, our earnest desire is not satisfied.

3077

WHY should we lengthen out this business? You should explain things to me in my own house. What a huge entanglement this is! You have made much of little. I shall lay my head at your feet; what will this cost you? This will free me, be assured, from debts due by or to me. Since the decision rests with you, why should we bring disgrace on ourselves? Thus the knot that bound us is untied. Tukā says, It is pleasant to come to a decision; when I see thee face to face, my delight in thee will much increase.

3078

I CANNOT believe, O Cowherd, that you will make it your rule to let your hair fall in disorder on your forehead and turn away from beggars. I cannot believe that God will follow a new course alike this. Tukā says, There never was any such delay as this, O Viṭṭhala.

3079

BE it due to my destiny, or that things are at an end with me, I know not; though I stand waiting at the door, no voice comes forth to me. What would it cost him to speak? He is a sluggard by nature, a sluggard from his earliest days. Tukā says, How can I show him any reverence in future?

3080

SOME countenance he ought to show us, else how can we put any confidence in him? Though I call myself his slave, how can I pass as such, unless my master looks on me face to face? Whom can I hold responsible for the days I have wasted, the days I have spent heedlessly? Till you show some purpose of your own, O God, says Tukā, I pray you, accept not my service.

3081

THE bliss of devotion I have not yet attained; I would fain see thy face with my own eyes. O Nārāyana, knowest thou not this desire of my heart? Thou hidest a sweetmeat in one hand, and showest thy child the other empty; thy majesty is not comely to behold so long as there goes not with it love for thy offspring. Even as a child, though he has sense, shows himself forward to his mother, so is it with me, O Pānduranga, says Tukā.

3082

THOU hast many to save and I have no refuge except thee. Bear thy task as best thou mayest; what else is there for thee to do? It will not look well if thou givest one of the row food and spurnest another. Tukā urges thee vehemently; thou hast too long forgotten him.

3083

HOW strong is the sense of self within me, if thou art not able to remove it! If this is so, who would fall at thy feet? Why art thou so niggardly of compassion? Is thy wealth wasted thereby? Tukā says, God ought to carry the bags of Self that belong to other men.

3084

THIS shows your bag is empty; you are stripped of everything, O Pānduranga! I have a full warehouse of my own at home; keep your own indifference to yourself! Tell me now, what have you left? I have brought you before all the world, to be my witness what I have done to you. Tukā says, Where will you look for your property? I am your master now.

3085

MY mind is drawn to protect you; I have forgotten myself. You must pay back what you have borrowed, neither more nor less. In my love for you, I renounced all my connections; I took my share of worldly censure. Even as my soul is drawn towards you, so on your side must the same disposition be seen.

3086

I AM treated with contempt; what have I to do with names or forms? No honour is shown to me, no message is sent for me. Taking thee to be my father and mother, I approached thee familiarly; but I found thou hast many relatives in the world. Tukā says, Now I will fold my hands and throw myself on the ground here where I am.

3087

I HAVE long been patient ; thou payest no heed to this, O Viṭṭhala ! Now I will seize thee by the hem of thy skirt; I will make myself thy peer. I am reckless of my life ; I stand up to encounter thee. Tukā begs the saints to tell this to the Lord of Pandhari.

3088

WHO has served thee for salvation and has not received some proof of thy power ? Tell me this, O generous Lord. This devotion to thee is an inheritance from generation to generation in my family. Who has not entreated thee for something else than knowledge of Bramhā ? Whose fond desires has thou not satisfied ? Whom, in ancient days, didst thou delay to save ? Tukā says, Why art thou changed ? Do I say anything without good evidence ?

3089

IF I knew the secret, I should not feel this weary pain. Our burden was on thy head ; what error could we make ? Hadst thou set us free from fear, our spirit would have been at rest. For something of this kind I am waiting, says Tukā ; I stand upright.

3090

I HAVE no sense of self left, or of my place as distinct from thine. Henceforth, O God, take thou good care of me, while I am with thee. Tukā says, If a wife has no clothes to wear, it will bring shame on her husband.

3091

HOW can a child petitioning endure this harsh treatment ? He feels ready to die. His parents ought not to see him in distress. Through the influence of the world, hitherto I have been kept far from you ; I have reached no eminent position at your feet. Tukā says, O God, keep me as thou wilt in any condition thou wilt.

3092

YOU should encourage your servants and make them feel confidence ; they will not fail to serve you well ; they will swell with pride in the dignity which your fondness bestows on them. They will rejoice in their master's words, in the hand on their head which sets them free from fear. They do not ask for extra wages, says Tukā ; but they feel sure these will be given them.

3093

WHETHER you command me to be saved or drowned I am ready ; this is my firm resolution. I cannot say if I was wilfully tormented by thee ; I shall receive in silence what thou givest me. Put an end to my petitioning, or at least bid me henceforth be thy servant. Whether I am to act or look on in silence, says Tukā, at least speak to me, O Pānduranga.

3094

THERE was once a child who cried for a cake such as he had never seen before. They placed a potsherd in his hand, and put an end to his fretting and grumbling. O Merciful One, do not treat me so! It is a parent's duty to do good to their children, says Tukā.

3095

I CATCH the hem of thy garment; I make myself thy peer. I have grown reckless of my life; I stand up before thee. Tukā implores the saints to tell this to the Lord of Pandhari.

3096

HONOUR and a good name do not fail to cost something; the man who carries a purse has to meet demands upon it. Tukā says, You know all this. I am full of impatience; there is no patience in me.

3097

WHAT need you spend from your own purse that thus you seek to evade me? What pleasure have you in thus amusing yourself? Tukā says, You have laid aside your manifest form; now who will set us free?

3098

MEN pay back what they have borrowed; the sum borrowed decides the payment. In proportion, then, as my soul is drawn towards you, there should be a movement on your part, O Pānduranga!

3099

I HAVE settled my purpose, now I give it expression; if you mean to be my father, you must accomplish it. There is to-day an eager desire in my mind; I have given up putting off things. I know my own resolve; I will not take a veiled reply. Tukā says, Though I have had to remind you of my resolution, still you should be proud of it.

3100

MAKE good your own words; recognize that you and we are equal. If a man departs from his words, it is against him that complaints will be made. Tukā says, Not so will it be with you and us; you will be our intimate and our friend.

3101

WHO will help me to find comfort in thee? If thou wouldst be called Purifier of the Sinful, fence me round on all sides. If not, give up the badge of thy claim. Fulfil your promises, then people will respect you. Take your part in the world out of respect for people's opinions; do not let your promises fail. Such is not the case with you and me, says Tukā; you will be my bosom friend.

3102

I LOOK wretched although I am thine; thou seemest to be even proud of this, O God! When a mother is angry with her infant child, who will help him in his distress? Just so, Vitho, without thy help I am a stranger in the land; do not cast me into this distress. My hopes are wholly centered on thee, says Tukā.

3103

THE Baudhya incarnation has fallen to my lot; his mouth has accepted the rule of silence. For people of former ages he assumed his blue colour and four-armed shape; but he speaks in secrecy to the saints of to-day. The Kali age has fallen to my lot; though I direct my gaze everywhere, you do not meet my eyes. What harm have I done to you, O Nārāyana? For whom have you no pity? says Tukā.

3104

THY character as Purifier of Souls thou dost not display in our case. If we suffer the pangs of birth and death, what does it profit thee? Tukā says, You have played truant with me, but I have seized your top-knot—your name.

3105

SEE, Pānduranga has played truant with me; but I have seized his top-knot—even his name. Let the saints now judge between us, who shows himself shameless here. Who is the wrong-doer here, O ye saints? We sinners do shout aloud his name. Make him renounce the name of Purifier; in truth, it is we who purify ourselves of our sins. We, no doubt, are the transgressors; but what avail us the tales told of *him* purifying men? Tukā says, Though we perish, we shall not quit your feet, O ye saints!

3106

TELL us what sin we have committed from which there is no escape. A deer and a fox received places in Vaikunṭha; what right had they to this? He who assailed the elephant in the pond —Hari asked him not if he was fit to be saved. Tukā says, Ganikā was vile, yet my troubles are greater than hers.

3107

THERE is a plant called the sun-plant; yet no light falls from it. Another is called, on Dasra day, the golden-tree; yet nobody would accept it as a pledge. Tukā says, O God, renounce your name and claims!

3108

IF the Ganges went to the sea, and he refused to give her a place, where could she go? Iṣ the water vexed with creatures that live in the water? Does a mother refuse to shelter her children? Tukā says, I have come to seek your protection; why are you silent?

3109

O SEA of mercy, O Lord of men, vindicate now the glory of thy name, the high claims of thy titles! In this Kali age, God has assumed his Baudhya manifestation; O, do not incur the censure of the world! Lo! the Kali age seeks to sweep away mother and son together; what have you to do with the wild tricks of the world?

3110

THOUGH I am a calf of the heavenly cow, I get no food to eat; what shall I do? Thus you have treated us, O Viṭṭhala; how is it you have forsaken us?

3111

WHERE are you detained by the meditations of yogis or the joyous preachings of Pandhari? What occupation engages you, that you cannot hear my complaints? Are you blissfully asleep on your serpent-bed? How is it you refuse the pleasure of listening to your worshippers? Tell me where you are detained, says Tukā.

3112

A MORTAL man, a food-eating worm, if you call yourself his servant, will not neglect you; he will not depart from his word. But *you* are the Lord of men, the Source of the sun and moon; you are the Feeder of the universe; you are extolled by the lord of snakes, says Tukā.

3113

SHALL I go through the penance of five fires or suffocate myself in smoke? Tell me, what pilgrimage shall I undertake? Where is your village? Let me run to it. What conduct shall I observe, what vow shall I undertake to make you merciful to me? You have turned harsh towards me; you give me no answer, says Tukā.

3114

THOU shouldest feel some shame for those that have clasped thy hand. Foul and feeble am I, but be thou merciful to this poor wretch. If a mother has a child with a running nose, does she not love him? Tukā says, Be assured, I will quit my body for thee.

3115

IF we call ourselves thine, then thou wilt be blamed when we fall short. That a man who has drunk nectar should die—is this in accordance with divine law? Beneath the tree of wishes, need beggars keep their bags tied up? When a man has found the magic stone, says Tukā, need he die of hunger?

VIII.—Prayers

3116

THOU hast drawn this body to thee; now make good use of it. O thou that knowest all, know this, that I know not what worship is. When a mother conceives a child, she understands all the signs belonging to it. Bear me on thy hip, O Hari, says Tukā.

3117

WHEREVER I look, there I see God—give me some such faith as this! I have grown attached to one spot; I am full of ideas about qualities good and bad. Wherever my head lies, let it lie at thy feet; do thou bring it to pass that my life may not be wasted. Tukā says, Sweep away all that keeps me from thee; take up thy dwelling-place at my feet.

3118

HEREAFTER, thou shouldest go with me wherever I go; thou art now turned into all my capital; now do not keep me from thy feet. Henceforth, O God, says Tukā, entangle me in no snare elsewhere.

3119

SHOULD the body fail to control itself, what are we to do? Fix, O fix my thoughts on thy feet. Suffer not the impulses of my mind to stray. Tukā says, If men act thus, blest are they to have been born.

3120

WHAT do we owe to one who gives us a perishable boon? Do not serve us up such counterfeits; give us the reality, O Viṭṭhala! Is she truly a mother who leaves her child crying behind her? Tukā says, Those are truly pious deeds that make thy fame to spread.

3121

ERE now, thou hast protected many in distress; thou runnest when they utter thy name in extremity. But me thou hast forgotten, O Pāndu-ranga. I am dying, says Tukā; spring forth to save me, O Keshi, my Lord!

3122

MY purpose is settled; I shall not change; I shall not leave the way I have found. Thou, then, must protect me; thy feet are all the strength of my mind. Should I say this in many ways, it will not grow plainer; we must each be the other's witness, mind to mind. O Life of my soul, says Tukā, O Nārāyana, thou art my witness.

3123

LET the Generous One fill up any deficiency; my intelligence is small, and I am at fault.

3124

I KNOW the due season, but my intelligence avails me nothing. It is thou who must thoughtfully teach me all. The mere asking of thee costs us nothing and saves us from all care. Tukā says, Bear with me; I am grasping thy feet.

3125

ONE standing at thy temple, like a door-keeper, entreats thee; save the suppliant from anxious care! All is known to thy feet.

3126

I CANNOT forbear to speak of the spot where my love dwells. The form that up till now has been brought before me, O take not that away! Hateful, O Nārāyana, says Tukā, is any course of life apart from thee.

3127

AT last, now I entreat thee, uttering just what is in my heart. I ask that thy name may be ever in my throat; this alone will fulfil my desires. Tukā says, So long as this wretched body holds together, so long shall I sing thy greatness.

3128

TUKĀ says, I feel that at such a season thou shouldest run to help me.

3129

IN many a birth I have come and gone; now do thou set me free. I am carried away by the stream of illusion; do thou stem the current and save me. Tukā says, Who but thou can save me from affliction?

3130

MAKE me thy own; give me this assurance — 'Fear not!'

3131

WITH outstretched hands, I run towards thee.

3132

TAKE care of the gift I have given thee; my intellect is now composed, I feel no desire for pleasure. Obstacles arise and keep men from thy feet; but, O may our union, says Tukā, be sweet from first to last!

3133

TAKE me by the arm, and lead me beyond the world. Thou art the chief jewel of the wise, a very mine of all attributes. Thou art the crest-jewel of all men, O blessed Viṭṭhobā! Make thyself a shining lamp, and banish our darkness. Rend the net desire, and take up thy dwelling in my heart. See how I am ensnared in my ignorance; pray, take thou thought for me! O Infinite One, Tukā lays his head on thy feet.

3134

THIS alone is the favour thou shouldest show us—to let us lay our burden upon thee. When hungry, men cry out for food; when they are cold, they need clothing. Whenever a desire arises within us, at once we cry to thee for what we want. Let not sorrow visit our house; keep thy *chakra* whirling round it. Tukā says, I desire not liberation; I would rejoice to be born into the world.

3135

WHAT shall I ask? Of whom shall I ask it? He of whom I should ask is near me. Were I to ask for Indra's habitation, even that is not eternal. Should I ask for Dhruva's habitation, Dhruva himself longs for the earth. Should I ask for the joys of Svarga, when my merit is exhausted, I must return here again. Should I ask for immortality, the soul is already, by its own nature, beyond death. Tukā says, There is but one thing I ask for—unbroken unity with thee!

3136

THE child must tell his longings to his parents; who else will minister to his fancies? Forgive me my mischievous acts; since I am near thee, why dost thou neglect me? Others than thou may gain dominion over me; where will thy greatness be then? Tukā says, I have approached thee from afar; keep aloof from me no more.

3137

MY eyes are wide-open, gazing intently, while a very Ganges of tears pours from them. Tukā says, Prove now thy truthfulness by carrying out thine original word.

3138

WHAT knows the child of its mother's mind? All care concerning him is borne by her. They are to each other as a stone is to a gourd—when the gourd keeps the stone afloat. So too does a snake coil itself round the trunk of a sandal-tree; it coils itself, but does not assume the nature of the tree because it is close to it. Now, do thou take the part of the magic stone, says Tukā, and consider me as iron.

3139

POUR down streams of nectar; put this child to your breast.

3140

I AM impatient for thy bounty; I have joined my palms together to receive it. Turn and cast thy merciful glance upon me; bring these things within my own experience. Thou art master, I, servant. There is a mutual agreement between us. Tukā stands before thee, face to face, and entreats thee.

3141

BID us perform for thee some service in thy presence; we will refuse wealth and houses, we will give up our lives for thy sake. Let us talk to each other, that our comfort may increase; let us gaze upon thy holy face. Tukā says, I speak the truth; let thy feet be my witness.

3142

COME, O Keshāva, for the sake of this helpless being.

3143

A QUARREL has sprung up among my members; they say, The ears and the tongue have their fill, while the hands and the feet and forehead are restless and the eyes are famished. My mouth sings thy attributes, my ears listen; but, say the other members, such is not our case. The sight of thee alone can gratify all, whereby each shall receive his own portion. Bestow this upon me, then, says Tukā; this is my desire.

3144

THOU showest thyself harsh to us; this is why I address thee. Thou knowest everything thyself. Thou sittest with a store of all merchandise before thee in one establishment; there is nothing there that belongs to any one else. Tukā says, There is everything at thy feet; O do not disappoint us!

3145

TAKE such measures that I may enjoy this company. Tukā says, I came to show my confidence that thou wouldest destroy the store of my past.

3146

NOTHING separates a mother from her child; there is no wearisome discussion between them. Give, O give me the sweets I crave for, in fond pity for one in trouble. Admiring thee for kindness such as this, I spoke the words I have spoken, O mother Pānduranga, says Tukā.

3147

WHY should I merely set my affection on thee? Let me sit by thy side and eat with thee. Assuredly, I will leave nothing uneaten; I swear so by thyself. I will closely examine the various dishes I have seen with thee. Tukā says, All the Cowherd's children have told me the tale of his doings.

3148

THY dwelling-place makes fear afraid; if thou art angry with us, where can we go? Tukā seeks a multitude of gifts from thee.

3149

WHEN a child is fondly loved, his father shows him no harshness in speech; nay, he saves him from harm when occasion arises. Thou hast brought thy servants from afar and dealt kindly with them; thou hast cherished them carefully. Thou hast suffered no wind of misfortune to blow on them; for harsh words wither them up. Tukā says, O merciful Hari, give us peace by words sweet as nectar.

3150

DO not chase away the dog that waits at thy feet; do not lift up thy hand against him. I have made myself a mere carcass, a very lout. O Life of the world! Observe thy pledges towards me, says Tukā.

3151

O LORD of the senses, mighty art thou! Why dost thou delay to speak? Expound this matter to me. Say thou 'Thus it is,' and I will arise and touch thy feet. Accepting thy words with joy, Tukā will dance in fond admiration.

3152

NOW it seems thou wilt show me thy true form, according to my desire. Therefore my resolution will not fade away; I have kept my eyes open. I am watching for thy face; I am waiting to see if time enough has passed. Tukā says, May I know what I shall gain, and when I shall gain it?

3153

THOU art rich and fortunate; I am full of impatient desire. Cursed is a life of expectation; in our wretched poverty, we gaze eagerly towards thee. Rescue me from this condition; give me experience, O God! Tukā says, When we have become one, then this misery will subside.

3154

WAS it because the appointed day had come, that thou didst suffer once so much toil and care? Thou didst carry out thy promise then; so my mind is drawn towards it. O Mother, thou knowest well thy children's fond desire; let no hardness of heart stand between them and thee. Tukā says, It is for us to speak, for you to make good our words.

3155

I KNOW not why things are like this now; the thoughts of those days thou hast suppressed. Tell us why thou hast set us on, to perform for thee ceremonies of devotion. Thou hast drawn our eyes towards thee; this has sunk and settled in our minds. Tukā says, Thou hast made this a habit of ours; O Cowherd bestow a gift on us full speedily!

3156

REMOVE from my path those snares which would lead me to destruction. Listen to my complaints; to my tales of grief and joy. Thy feet are the only place we have where we can pour out our feelings. Tukā says, We, creatures of thy womb, are thy burden, O God.

3157

IN the strength of thy name, I toil through time. I have been oppressed by many enemies ; day and night, I live in fear of them. Seat thyself, says Tukā, at the root of my mind ; the net of evil will be loosed from off me.

3158

IF thou doest something now, let it be something truly done ; give me the gift of grace I have asked for. They say thy promises are never violated; thou knowest the difference between sin and merit. Ample is thy power over the earth ; this claim of thine is loudly announced. Tukā says, O Consort of Rakumai, why dost thou consider me an encumbrance ?

3159

SEND down upon us a shower, for my soul is athirst. I look up to the sky in hope ; thou knowest it, thou whose abode is the world. Thus, through union with thee, the germ that is within me will grow and be reared up. The fruit, says Tukā, will be the full-blown lotuses of thy feet.

3160

THIS forgetfulness ought not to steal over me so often ; I should be filled inwardly with thy attributes. The attraction of wealth fills my mind with impatience ; but no less impatient should I be to meditate on thy feet. Tukā says, O moisten my soul with moisture of life ; bestow it on me speedily, O Pānduranga !

3161

THE greatest gain that birth brings us is the sight of the lotus-naveled God. How can I cast off the encumbering cloak of life ? I have travelled hither by many stages ; I have lived in fear of yon dreadful place. Tukā says, O mother mine, Viṭṭhala, come to me in my last hour !

3162

HE suffers no stains of guilt to cling to me ; he wipes them off constantly, as occasion arises. O thou that dwellest near me, run, I pray thee ; release me from these stains. Whatever comes to light within me, I disclose ; thou, hearing my cries, runnest to me.

3163

BY bodily toil, I have reached this unattainable spot; think now, O Nārāyana, what careful treatment to bestow on me. I am oppressed by debts ; thou must pay them off. Tukā says, I am feeble, so I come to thee with entreaties.

3164

I WANDERED much from place to place ; my faith was never sufficient for me. Yet peace I did at last obtain ; I survived, and now I say,

Accept, O God, my blessing; be happy in the good fortune we bring thee. Tukā says, Let us first begin our meal, and then eat the pungent dishes in the middle of it.

3165

NOW, why should I feel any impatience? He on whom this care rests must bear it. I shall not trouble to win myself fame; I desire not to be learned in the Scriptures. Tukā says, Being now under the inspiration of God, I need not go anywhere.

3166

ENSNARED as we are by hope, we entreat thy mercy; our soul is fully devoted to its aim. Keep me by thee in such estate as thou seest fit; cut me off from the world, and make me a mendicant. Tukā says, When a decree is given, who can go on prating?

3167

AFTER much scrutiny, this statement I make; I present my entreaties at thy feet. O Consort of Kamalā, disappoint me not! Oblations of Ganges-water offer thou to the Ganges, even to Pānduranga. Tukā folds his hands and makes obeisance.

3168

SPEAK to me and clear away this blackness from my soul; I shall see then the delicate lotuses of thy feet. O Soul of my soul, says Tukā, draw aside the curtain that hides me from thee!

3169

THE experience of great saints shall enter my soul; my soul pants eagerly for this bliss. Now take thou my soul as an oblation to thyself; give me a place in the ranks of the saints. My speech is like a creeper that spreads itself out but bears no fruit; it is barren, and dry like chaff. Tukā says, I am come to the last extremity; do not leave me, O Nārāyana, in the rear of the other saints.

3170

THOU knowest what will lead to my true welfare; inflict on me no craze that will ruin me. All power is thine; so likewise all knowledge. Prince of the wise, call Tukā thine own!

3171

I HAVE called myself thine; before whom else should I stand? It would not look well in me to go elsewhere. Time has long been pursuing me; he will not let me stand with steady purpose before thee. Bear not in mind my store of merits past; to purify the sinful is thy part. Tukā says, I marvel that others should have power to control me so long as I am praying to thee.

3172

'SAVE me'! 'Save me'! 'Save me'! Spare me now those cries; let my love cling to thy feet.

3173

GIVE me thy embrace with overflowing love; let my generous master cool my limbs. Rain down upon me the nectar of thy glance. Raise me up, and ask if I am hungry or thirsty; wipe my face with thy saffron robe. Take me by the chin and caress me; wave the neem-leaves round me, and protect me from the evil-eye. Tukā says, Show me, O Father, some such kindness as this!

3174

TUKĀ says, With single-hearted faith, I lay my fainting spirit at the feet of all.

3175

I STAY by thy feet to do my duty there. If thou meanest to do what is right, save a sinful man, says Tukā.

3176

I AM ever wondering when thou wilt send a messenger to call me. I have long been restless; I have long carried the burden of my body. Lift now this load off me, says Tukā; take me upon thy hip, O Pānduranga.

3177

STROY not the life of r erring child.

3178

THOU art the store of my past, the whole of my merit, my inheritance, O Pānduranga! Thou art my good deeds, my duties done, my daily vows, O Nārāyana! I wait for a gracious word from thee; Tukā says, O most beloved of loving beings, O best of beings, speak to me!

3179

TUKĀ says, Advise me as an elder; whom else, O Sea of mercy, can I consult but thou?

3180

MORE of such happiness I ask in future; a gift of service to thee bears fruits of joy.

3181

BEFORE whom else, say, shall I open my mouth? Who else knows my inner mind? As I come and go, I look towards thee; consider this, O Pānduranga! Fear, anxious care, and all occupations I have renounced; I remember thy feet alone. Forget me not; thus Tukā, thy humble bard, entreats thee.

3182

AS is the faith I show to the world, such is the space within me. As is the gem, says Tukā, such is its lustre when it is set in gold.

3183

THROUGH the attractive power of life, the mind is filled with hopes; a love of names and forms grows up within it. Have we no treasure prepared for us at thy feet? Why are my words so falsified? Tukā says, Pass over all my qualities; vindicate thine own name.

3184

WHEN a faun loses itself in the forest, its heart breaks with grief; so I, without thee, am a stranger in a strange land; do not wait to see me perish. Take to thyself the millions of sins I have committed; do not disappoint me at the last. Give a thought to me now, O Infinite One, says Tukā.

3185

HEAR now my last prayer. O Lord of Kamalā! Body, speech, and mind I have surrendered at thy feet. Now my soul and the Soul Supreme ever dwell in union in my heart; stay for ever in my throat, O Keshāva!

IX.—The conditions of acceptation

3186

IN that case, the seed within should be true and pure. Tukā says, When the smallest particle of salt drops into water, it turns salt.

3187

IN many a life, I carried on this quest; now, I have come by this portion. Now I shall sacrifice my life, and burn up my wordly interests. When once they are gone, methinks no anxious care will trouble me. Tukā says, Come, let us hasten to grasp Viṭṭhala's feet.

3188

GOD does not suffer his worshipper to follow any worldly vocation; he himself winds up his affairs. If God gave him wealth, he would be puffed up; so he brings him to beggary. If he gave him a virtuous wife, unreal desires would entangle him; so he sets a shrew upon him. Observe, says Tukā, such has been my own experience; why need I say more?

3189

THIS is the sum of all: cast your burden upon God, and live like a beggar that solicits no alms. Entrust your body to God, but employ its strength in due season yourself. Be well assured, He who nourishes the world will support and extend it. Know that his strength alone is needed, says Tukā.

3190

I HAVE vowed to myself that in very truth I will be thy servant. I will betake myself to thy feet, to Pandhari, the root of all. Till then, I am but filling my belly with food; I have been raising a futile clamour. I have not found the true path; I am wandering at random. We ought to live a life of respect; this will make the Lord favourable to us. Men who keep their promises find out what friendship is. Now let things happen as they will; my father and mother control everything. Tukā says, What anxiety is there now? I have a port to look to.

3191

THE wife makes a vow to secure her husband's return to his village; what merit is there in her action? She makes a vow for her own benefit,—that her children may grow up, and she may have a house full of wealth and food. To expect merit in such a case, would be to demand flint for the magic stone, or to spend money in buying arsenic, says Tukā.

3192

FOR him who loves Hari's name the net of illusion is broken, the sea of the world is scattered. Who is so strong that he has passed it in this age by dint of actions or duties done? We cannot learn by heart the Veda, or grasp the sense of the Scriptures; master, then, the roll of his names.

3193

CULTIVATE that wealth which all men desire; which is more than enough both to eat and to give, which measuring cannot exhaust. If such a seed be sown deeply, in a moist place, then the crop will come into your hands. Tukā says, The three letters bring this contentment.

3194

IT is mere cowardice in those that will not take the step; Nārāyana stands upright, ready to welcome them. He has made the sea of life a mere puddle; all you need do is to call on him. Take, step by step, the path leading to him; then, what can arrest you? Tukā says, He pays no heed to true or false, to great or small.

3195

ILL-STARRED is he who sets off on the path to a holy place; the very place he reaches becomes an obstacle to him. The best plan, therefore, is to sit still in one place, with one's thoughts fixed on the root of the mind. To rely on plans is to trust oneself to destiny; one action brings on another, and that, another. Tukā says, Pleasure has not one face alone; you will find happiness by suppressing it.

3196

WHETHER you know your duty or not, listen, I will tell it you; utter zealously the name of Viṭṭhobā. He will show you pathways, straight pathways, such as you need. He is full of abundant mercy; all you need is devoted love to him. As long as we asked others concerning the way, we made many mistakes; but we have now with us an honest guide, one who won't let thorns pierce us or thieves carry off our belongings. Tukā says, There is nothing to pay him but the words Viṭṭhobā! Viṭṭhobā!

3197

THE faithful believes he need not exert himself; the mood comes over him unbidden. The mother asks her child for a morsel; when he gives it her, she feels an eager joy. She takes a pride in his lisping words; she quotes them, and wears them like an ornament. Tukā says, This can all be proved; Pānduranga himself will take my side.

3198

WE will give a taste of our experience to those who are ready for it; we will empty our bags before those who will prize their contents. The withered flowers offered to God, should you string them along with jewels, will nevertheless shine by their own lustre. The first thing needed is the essence of faith; *that* is the good soil; with that you need not be anxious about seed or crop. Tukā says, If a thing has good qualities of its own, you need not spread its fame abroad.

3199

HOW you lower yourself by abusing your fellow-men! The riddle of the world has altogether degraded you. Seek shelter in my Lord; he keeps his faithful close to him. Your proper course is to ask nothing of him; to do the work appointed you to do—provided it is not done through any sort of desire. Tukā says, Devotion will carry you to the goal, if you keep your soul intent on service alone.

3200

NOW I am waiting for this to be given me; I make no efforts to obtain it. I need not scrutinize my store of merit to see if it be enough. Tukā says, I will render him such service as he finds agreeable.

3201

WITH us pure devotion alone survives; we have no use for skill or knowledge. Pānduranga, my Lord, possesses all knowledge; he, Gopāla, presses my body to his. Tukā says, This we cannot attain by actions performed or duty done; only the faithful can make it their own.

3202

LOVE gives us power to control others; the parents fear their own child. He cannot actually use force to them; but he uses entreaties and sets up a cry. He clings to their dress, and tumbles about them till he hurts them. Tukā says what he likes, and Viṭṭhala puts up with it.

3203

THE street-juggler may play the part of Nārāyana by making himself up for it; but he remains a juggler after all. Men give the name 'God' to a stone, and faith in it can save a man; yet it remains what it was. You might call the *dhatura* 'the Golden Tree,' and place it on your head to honour it; but it would not take rank among your possessions. Tukā says, It is a man's faith that saves him; the sense of self destroys him.

3204

A MAN loves one man, and in his own mind dislikes another. God has bestowed various dispositions on men; there are various grades of them,—high, medium, and low. The difference we make between them depends on the love we feel towards them; some we honour, some we censure. Only, says Tukā, if you love God, does God feel an affection for you.

3205

THIS is sport to you, but death to us; we have endured much trouble and many a re-birth. Now I will take such steps that thou wilt visit us thyself; I will utter thy name. Apart from thee, I have passed through wild forests, carrying a burden of projects in my mind. Tukā says, Now I have found an easy key; till now, I was entangled in sin and merit.

3206

WE listen to the glorious deeds of the Infinite; they who had the name of Hari in their thoughts, they have crossed the stream of life, they have snapped the fetter of the world. Now, slowly let us pass along the same path, with such right as we may have to do so. They anchored their boats here, and went on; no jealousy of theirs bars our way; we have no price or freightage to pay; single-minded faith is enough. Tukā says, He is waiting for us upright, on even feet; he has made a wharf on the Bhima's bank; rise up, move on speedily.

3207

IF a man keeps within him his private purpose,—were it as small as a sesamum-seed,—or sense of self, Nārāyana will not draw near him.

3208

TRUTH is one and the same thing with renunciation; we need not spend words over this. Nārāyana's servants are like himself; this is the desire on each side. When the mind is free from all uncleanness, then God comes to rule it. Tukā says, Know that this is the voice of a good man that speaks.

3209

THIS is a part of a speaker's art—not to let another appear stronger than he; he has to show himself stubborn, just as we, O God, are stubborn in dealing with you. We must make our way into your heart; we must reach the bottom of it by throwing ourselves at your feet. Tukā says, By our own words, we must bring you round to a gracious mood.

3210

WHEN we have fixed our eyes on some clear aim, no hesitation arises in the mind. A brave man stalks proudly across a battle-field; he delights in death. What is needed is yearning love; then our strength will not fail. Tukā says, If a man has a generous heart, his mind will not fail him.

3211

WHAT keeps us from thee is this: our sense of self parts us. God has shown us this secret truth, and dispelled all illusion. It is as though a man should twist his own ear; the pain he suffers is much the same. Tukā says, While we enjoy the bliss of solitude, all the congeners of the body are bound up there together with it.

3212

WHEN we possess such a secret as this, why should we be ignorant and lost in confusion. I will grasp his feet, and embrace him as he stands; I will not let him stir. I will contract my desires, and fix my eyes on his glorious face. Tukā says, I have forsaken the multitude of doctrines; I hold with a firm grasp the one thing sufficient for me.

3213

NOT by knowledge or reflection canst thou be comprehended; nor can any system search thee out. Thou art not to be found in the depths of the Scriptures; the Vedas cannot express the limits of thy nature. Tukā says, Thou hast no finite bounds; so my own thoughts about thee end in failure.

3214

MY soul is weary of the pleasures of the world. I have no friend but thee. When shall I see that beauteous form, and cling to it with a fond, loving embrace? How can I gain this end without any aid from my past? Gopāla's humble servant, Tukā, entreats him.

3215

AS long as you trust to your lock of hair and your sacred thread, you are the slave of Vedic texts. If you fail to keep the rules they prescribe, you will fall into sin and go down to hell. Astute and wise though you may be, take care you keep the rules in all their integrity. Break off with the lock and thread, then nothing more will encumber you. Tukā says, Only when you behave as though the world were stranger to you, only then will signs of Bramha come to light in you.

3216

IF we surrender all, then only are we truly united to God ; otherwise, he will only give to each an experience proportioned to his desires. Each will receive according as he gives, so it is your soul that must go. Tukā says, The best plan is to keep nothing back.

3217

WHAT ought I to know or not to know ? I will grasp thy feet in my mind. What ought I to do or to leave undone ? By faith I will imprison theee in my heart. I ask, O God, says Tukā, to serve thee from birth to birth.

3218

MEANS of salvation require excessive toil ; let me only sing to thee with heart-felt faith ; I shall gain everything while I am seated there. The slave of God can perform acts of ritual or charity ; his body and mind are motionless. Tukā says, When a man is one with the Supreme, all stirrings of the mind cease.

3219

IF God shows me any favour, then the knowledge I receive will be Bramha itself. There will be no need to bring anything from anywhere, or to go anywhere to get salvation. If a man gives God a place in his mind, his mortal eyes will become divine. Tukā says, When God manifests himself, there will be no room for an individual soul anywhere.

3220

KNOWLEDGE acquired from the sight of others—what is the use of it, so long as we have no experience of our own? The pleasures of the senses have led many astray; later on, when they would fain give them up, they cannot repress them. A well-planned diet, righteous dealings with men, freedom from passion—these are the means of salvation. As when a ship is anchored on the sand and a gale assaults it, so is it with the pompous self-conceit of man. Tukā says, Control your mind till you grasp Narayana.

3221

IF you wish to churn milk, there are things you must do and things you must not do; this is the secret of butter. You must not spoil the process, or all the butter will disappear. You must take care of what rises to the surface; you must not let the essence be lost. Tukā says, When you have satisfied your hunger, then you should lick your fingers.

3222

OUR mouths should be saints themselves, our senses religious ascetics; I know of nothing else that is truly faith or devotion. These are the only two divine songs; all others are sung merely for amusement. Tukā assumes a posture of the mind, and sings God's praises.

3223

I HAVE made myself strong by descending to be a suppliant. I have entered his house, and brought a treasure home with me. I have arranged my plans so as to win a treasure of my own. Tukā says, I embraced his feet, and plundered all his wealth.

3224

THE lisping of a child, whatever it be like, pleases the mother well. Sweet is the love of a child; that is why she likes his words. The child runs before and behind her; he pulls and pushes her, but she puts up with it all. Is it not so, Pānduranga? Tukā entreats you to say.

3225

WHEN we attain to a mortal body, we should consider its essential purpose; we should persevere on the road to devotion. We should confine the restless mind to one spot, and humble ourselves at the feet of the saints. With full assurance, we should clasp the hand of faith; the fears of life will then disperse to other lands. Save the name, there is no easy path on earth; sing forth his name with joy. Blessed is the man who does this, says Tukā; he has become a very Meru of fixed resolution.

3226

OUR innumerable doctrines are fabrications of words; by committing them to memory, men grow voluble. The secret of my Viṭṭhobā is far removed from them; as long as they are possessed by the senses of the body, how can Viṭṭhobā enter them? Sacrifice and penance, thought and things thought of, fail to reach him. Tukā says, When we grow weary of the world, we conceive a passion for him.

3227

IF a man has no spare time, and still bears in mind the Wielder of the Disc, he will help him. When the soul is deeply agitated, should a man fix his thoughts on Pandhari, Nārāyana will help him. If he has no bodily strength, let him offer nothing but faith; the prince of Pandhari will help him. Whether you have strength or not, even though you be the slave of others, still be not heedless of him. If a man thinks of him, says Tukā, Nārāyana approaches him.

3228

THOUGH the hands and feet should join forces and say, 'Come let us use our own eyes to see with,' still, since they have no sight, how could they see? The eye alone is the beholder of all things. When the Eye of the eye went forth to see, says Tukā, he stood alone and continued to gaze.

X.—The necessity of experience

3229

THE joy of devotion no others know, be they learned, or Vedic readers, or men of information. Those who, by rapt contemplation of the self, have not their own souls free, even they cannot compass the bliss of devotion. If Nārāyana shows his mercy, says Tukā, then only can we master this secret.

3230

LOOK at my experience; I have made God my own. I need only speak what he puts into my mouth, at any time when I answer you. Only when we quit this wicked world does Govinda become our bond-servant. I have taken the bold step, says Tukā; thus I have made him prisoner.

3231

BRING iron, cotton, and wool together, then fire leaps out when a blow is struck. Experience will enlighten the mind in its own season. Food brings the experience of satisfied hunger; let us set our desires on it, for this is the measure to take. Tukā says, When soul mingles with soul, then who can apply a name and when?

3232

GOD is bankrupt, he has lost everything. Why should I waste any more speech on him? I must approach him by my innermost mind. He has put up the shutters and lighted a lamp in his shop. Tukā says, O people, take steps to keep him in your house.

3233

CLEARLY has this knowledge shown itself—that Nārāyana is in all beings. You must make experience your own, by putting up a prayer to God. The voice utters speech according to what the eye sees or according to what falls on the ear. Tukā says, You should master the secret which will enable you to attain.

3234

THIS gift of my master's I have attained through the sight of him. Let us debate this in a spirit of love; let us hold a dialogue concerning your happiness. The only thing that will make this secret known is pious service at your feet. Tukā says, Bring this intelligence of mine to complete attainment.

3235

FIRE cannot be described or set forth; it is an experience of the mind which the mind alone understands. The young of the tortoise are fostered by the mother's kind glances; she suckles them not, but they cling to her in a fast embrace. Who teaches the snakes, while they are yet in the womb, to hide themselves as soon as they are born? Man may know well the difference between sweet and salt, though he cannot describe it; he knows well the feeling in his mind. Tukā says, Let the mind consider things well for itself; let not the good enquire of other men.

3236

WHEN you gather fragments of gold and melt them into a bar, the gold is just as it was; it is known as genuine gold, such as it was at first. It has passed the test of fire, the test of heat, and the test of filing and boring. You may take it round all the country, says Tukā, but you will not lose by it.

3237

A PARROT knows how to say what he has been taught; but what is there really in him corresponding to this knowledge? A man cannot become a prince through any pleasure that dreams bring him; my experience has shown me this. Why was my tongue graced with ornaments of speech? I seem only to drift farther from thy feet. A treasure beheld in a mirror we cannot grasp nor put in our purse; yet it looks to our eyes as though it was real. We go on hankering after it, but we have to gulp down our spittle; it seems to be a mere delusion. The gift of poetry confers sweetness on speech; this the Puranas testify. Tukā says, A cowherd keeps the cows of other men; he calls them his, but he gets no profit out of them.

3238

MY sight has brought me no experience; I speak only what my ears have heard. If you utter the word 'cakes,' what comes of it? Does it make you feel as though you had eaten a meal? O Hari and Hara, if you send friendly enquiries after me by letter, and show me no honour when we meet, what response must I think you mean to give me? Why are you not the same within and without? You act as though you were a stranger to me. You create hopes in us by crying 'I come,' then you let the drowning man drift down the stream. Tukā says, O Crest-Jewel of Wisdom, how long must I cry to you? Where are you?

3239

A BLIND man describes things as they are described to him; but a man who can see has the evidence of his eyes before him. When a man has an established dwelling-place, this shows that his fathers before him were powerful men. How can a feeble man find any comfort in life? Tukā says, Let us make ourselves a home by our own valour, then we can praise it to the world.

3240

HE who is truly loved by another finds a home near him; others, though they approach, are still left far away. A cow deserts a full-grown calf, though it be of her own family. The lover alone knows the sweetness of his mistress's love, though others may find pleasure in her company. Tukā says, Speak where your words will be truly valued.

3241

YOU cannot cook your food backwards; you must follow the rules which have been laid down. You cannot trust the words of a great talker; they are mere chaff, with no taste in them. How can a man gather fruit before he plants a tree? A man who jests about doing so, you may call an idle prater. How many wretches have been cheated in this way, says Tukā; they imagine that wheat itself tastes like cakes.

3242

SUCH is so-and-so, the voice may be compelled to say; but the mind's experience should tell it, 'He is not such.' The body loves bodily actions; for thus within and without come to correspond with each other. When a mother and son meet unexpectedly, tears depart from them because of the joy they feel. Tukā says, One thing reveals the other; good brings good to light; mere show ends in mere show.

3243

MUSK-DEER carry in themselves the odour of musk; but though it belongs to them, they are not conscious of it. Lucky men buy it for a price; but the deer, who carry it as a burden, are killed for its sake. The *chakora* bird satisfies its thirst with the nectar of the moon; the bee feeds on sweet odours. Experts gain their knowledge from examples like these; even as a jewel is appreciated by the jeweller's eye. What would be the use of putting it in a blind man's hand? It would be wasted, as a pearl would be wasted, says Tukā.

XI.—Triumphant Happiness

3244

THE best of all places, a scene of delight, is any place where you remember God's feet. Be it a forest or a house, lonely or crowded, there the spirit is at peace. Blessed is that time, a very stream of joy, which is spent in contemplating Govinḍa. Be assured, says Tukā, by the aid of Nārāyana, that is a time of true gain, a time of good fortune, a halcyon time.

3245

THROUGH the power of our master, everything is humbled before us; Time and Death are subject to us. God is proud of his servants; so, offering to him all our aspirations, we rest at his feet. Let Nārāyana, says Tukā, fulfil our childish longings, and give us a plaything such as we desire.

3246

I FEEL as though I must dance, so fondly do I love thy nature. My limbs are set in motion; they are pulled by the strings of thy commanding power. Thy name and form have filled them with this passion; naturally do they follow this course they are entered on. Tukā says, Pānduranga embraces me.

3247

THIS bending and bowing to every one, the vexations of my husband's house, they are chased away; I shall see this misery no more. In her husband's house, a girl is the slave of many; but in a moment, says Tukā, that has all been uprooted and ended.

3248

I HAVE put on me, like an ornament, the pleasure of devotion; now let me taste this nectar. In the gatherings of the saints, we shall speed along the time, raising loud shouts of joy and love. Here, on earth, we have the very bliss that sets Bramha marvelling. We desire not Vaikunṭha; Pānduranga comes running to his service; why should we seek liberation? How can it bestow on us such a mood as this? Tukā says, This fulfils all my longings.

3249

ALL other pieces of good fortune would I wave round him and throw away; yes, were it such a lot as Indra's. I am confident, through my own experience, that God dwells in the house of Vishṇu's devotees.

3250

HE suffices even for the feeble.

3251

WHEN we have once made this strength our own, then we are free from anxious care. If once we have gained this happiness, we need nothing else.

3252

THERE is not a trace or bond left; the world has been made invisible to me. I need only sit and eat what God has freely given me. I am set free from fear; there is no room for any second in my heart. There is no reason, says Tukā, for me to add any more.

3253

WHY need we take this case before the court? It was settled when it began. The deed of gift is in my hands, bearing the signatures of many saints. I stayed by myself away from you, uttering the words 'mine, mine'; but at last the quarrel has been mended; there need be no more grumbling now. The treasure that was set apart has been put into my hands; you, O God, have no control over it now. Tukā says, All wrangling would be wasted now; I have taken possession of my own share.

3254

HE shines forth plainly, as huge as the world; all darkness is banished. There is no place where one could hide from it; for the world is laid open before us. The day of truth has dawned; words suffice not to describe its growth. Tukā says, I have surrendered my soul to you; I have embraced the Very Highest.

3255

WE have made ourselves strong by falling before you in supplication; we have made our way into the house and seized the store. We have planned things so as to gain possession of the treasure. We have embraced his feet, says Tukā, and thus we have set ourselves free.

3256

THE home of bliss, the fountain of joy welling up; the Lord whose glory it is that no one dare even look at his child; when he has a servant like himself, he will take him home with him. Tukā says, This is the gift bestowed on us by the Infinite Splendour.

3257

WHEN pleasure is added to pleasure, there follows, as it were, the curdling of milk, and butter is churned forth from it. The body trembles and sways with joy, the arms and eyes grows cool. This is the might of Nārāyana; through his attributes these properties in us are developed. Tukā says, The measure is heaped above the brim, so it runs over.

3258

THOU art rest for the weary; I wave neem-leaves and salt around thy name. O Joy Supreme, who receivest the forlorn and accountest them no burden. Tukā says, My desires are satisfied!

3259

WE were afraid because we spoke of 'ourselves'; but he has taken us on his own back. The whole world belongs to us now; Time is not left a particle of power over us. While we utter the name of the Mighty One, what anxiety can we feel? Tukā says, In Nārāyana our life is full of bliss.

3260

THERE is none that can prevail against him; what is there that the Lord of Pāndhari cannot accomplish? O mind of mine, what refuge is there for you to run to? Be now at peace. The power of the senses to draw you after them, the traffic of the world we have banished; all that penetrated you and set you in motion. Tukā says, We have conquered Time; we sit still.

3261

WE Vaishnāvas consider this the inherited religion of our race; we rely on this name with whole-hearted confidence. Then alone, you may call us servants of Hari and extol us, when first we have purified our minds of desire. We ask of thee neither the pleasures of the world nor liberation; we sing thy praises with love and joy, and dance before thee. Tukā says, Grant me from birth to birth this life to lead.

3262

GOD has grown friendly to me; he has satisfied my soul with sweet after sweet. I have secured a prosperous harvest; the stain on my soul is gone. Sins and merits have vanished with me; by one ablution, I have wiped them off.

Tukā says, My voice is purified in Janārdana who dwells in men.

3263

WE have been comrades from birth to birth; now, unexpectedly, we have met each other. Now the thread of love cannot be broken; though you let it go, it will not leave your hand. Tukā says, At last, you and I are truly united.

3264

HE called me to him and pacified my mind, by pouring out his sweets—the bliss of love. He strung together the gems of his names, and gave me them as a wreath to wear. This bliss, says Tukā, set me at my ease; I was engrossed in his name, and his name made me happy.

3265

SHE has fostered me in many lives and given me an eminent place at her feet. She let me form the habit of asking her for sweets I love. Tukā says, She never lets me feel, for a moment, separate from her.

3266

WHAT we lack, our mother provides and brings us, while she sings songs to comfort us. All pleasures come round to us where we are. Wherever we choose to stay, as our own inclinations prompt us, in that very spot we look our best. We have plucked up by the roots the tree of desire; all sinful wishes we have banished. Tukā says

Vitthala, the mother of her worshippers, will cast her shade upon us.

3267

THROUGH the power of our lord, the purposes of mortal men are attained. Since we have the power of God behind us, we bring Time into subjection. We can accomplish all with God to help us. Tukā says, Through the controlling power of our Lord, we need never more feel fear.

XII.—Raillery of God

3268

A FRIENDLY quarrel ends in no triumph of either side, though the words sound harsh. The father is grieved by his son's grief; they live with one life between them. Nothing can break the close bond of their love; no enmity can place a barrier between them. Tukā says, If I utter a piteous cry, the Cherisher of the Universe will draw near to me.

3269

O BEST of beings, there is no one to compare with you! Your intelligence is not master of itself; you cannot stay awake unless we call on you. If we wake you up, you manifest yourself. Tukā says, You need teaching every day.

3270

THE glory and excellence of thy name I have proclaimed; but I taste it not myself. How can peace abide with me? What I impose on myself does not dwell with me. We marvel at anything that brings us real gain; that is what we long for; traffic in the spurious ends in the spurious. Tukā says, Get thee glory for thyself; do not wait for pious service from me.

3271

LOVE didst thou bestow; an attentive mind didst thou require; an exchange took place between us. Why should we call thee generous? With trusting faith, thou takest one thing and givest another. Thou givest little and takest much; thou forbiddest all men to judge thee. Tukā says, Thou didst allot to us an attentive mind as our capital, and now thou hast cast us into an indifferent mood.

3272

WHEN a man is ready to sacrifice his life, why need he show any fear or deference towards anybody? You penniless wretch, I shall strip your blanket off you in the market-place! The more respect I show you, the more trouble you give me. Tukā says, I shall publish your origin and family.

3273

YOU take the souls of others, but you show them no pity. You will not give away your own superfluities; this is meanness, O Govinḍa! If we are to serve thee, at least we desire to see thy person; we cannot endure that thou shouldest hide thyself. Tukā says, O Master, O Destroyer of all things!

3274

THERE is a fell spirit that lives at Pandhari; it pounces on men who pass along the road. Go not there any of you; those who went there never came back. Tukā went to Pandhari; he came not back to life again.

3275

MY devotion you look on as a loan; as a pledge I hold your feet. Give me for interest your love, O Hari, and hasten to settle accounts between us. My other wealth I shall not give up,—my right to preach you continually. Your name is a bond that has passed between us; you are welcome to take me to court over it. O you that are borne on Garuḍa, my witness, says Tukā, is my teacher!

3276

IF we want to quarrel, let us quarrel with God and fix our thoughts on him; thus the best of men have told us. Why should *we* hide ourselves from God? If he will not meet us, he is welcome not to meet us. Let him enjoy his life of bliss in Vaikunṭha; he is welcome to keep us moving from land to land. If God has filled his heart with pride, there let him dwell by himself. As long as we grasp his name in our minds, we shall live happily here; we shall sing joyfully songs about

Govinda. Tukā says, This is God's way of letting things go astray; see, we rock ourselves to and fro with joy.

3277

YOU and I are kinsmen from of old; first we were relatives, then we were sons of one mother. Since we shared the estate between us, people do not respect us; but I have my own authority over the estate, and I shall exercise it. We became then sons of your daughter, your grandsons, and we lost the blest condition that we enjoyed before. I am the brother of your wife Lakshmī, a near relation, a defamer; hence it is that you deride me. We tease each other unbecomingly; 'twere better to say nothing of this. *You* will not recognize mother, sister, or daughter; the sin of their existence has been laid to our charge. The five senses have brought disgrace on us; we dare not show our faces to the world. Tukā says, We shall first grasp the root; what is to be done afterwards, we shall leave alone at present.

3278

SAY, whom did *you* save or carry to the further shore? It is the saints who convey to us words of instruction, then you give your assent to them. Tukā says, Not to you are we grateful; it is the saints whose names we utter.

3279

SO niggardly art thou, O Govinda, that thou wouldst not give away even thy superfluities.

This habit of thine we cannot understand. Thou requirest us to serve thee with all our members; if we cheat thee of one, thou canst not brook it. Since Tukā has renounced all action, why dost thou exact such toil from him?

XIII.—Faith and trust

3280

HE alone deserves the name of valiant who conquers the world; others are feeble creatures, pack-horses laden with selfish desires. But he is truly valiant who makes God his prisoner by faith. Best of all, says Tukā, is the life ever spent in his praises.

3281

THE son of Devaki has made me like himself, through contemplation of him. So he did with the cowherds too, riveting them to himself. When once he has taken us to himself, says Tukā, he does not leave us.

3282

THE child of a powerful man may play without fear; when *he* is arrayed in ornaments, they look well on him; with others, they are a burden that brings no honour. He may go anywhere he likes, because his father and mother are powerful. So it is with me, says Tukā; hence it is that I have offered thee my service.

3283

WHAT means the unrest of all this burden of worldly activities? My Lord knows the secret reason; my business is only to take my meals. The anxiety rests on the right head; the little child has only to play. Tukā says, This ends the matter; the person affected by these words is God.

3284

ONCE I was full of cares and desires; now they have been destroyed; once you were indifferent to me, and turned away from me as though I had been separate from you. The net of illusion increases misery, but the current is now drawing away both one and the other. What can now foster our desires? says Tukā.

3285

O THOU that standest on the brick, thou hast saved me all manner of trouble. Thou has averted from me birth and rebirth; who need be angry now and at whom? If we are to depend on plans formed by us, much toil will be needed before fruit is produced. Tukā says, Now, whether we are to meet or not, depends on your own passion for us.

3286

I AM born to die; yet I am contented with this very lot. I am delighted with it beyond all measure; I can never say 'Too much of it!' There has been a very fountain of nectar opened, whereof we can never have too much. Tukā says, The name of Viṭṭhala is relished in the mouth and is well digested afterwards.

3287

WHATEVER praises we bestow on you are really dispraise; they are fond expressions of ours; cherish them through the love you bear us. I amuse you with my prattle; I crave for sweets, says Tukā, with the innocent desire of a child.

3288

I ABHOR the world and its affairs, so I have given them up, and lie crouching down here. The illusion can return on me no more; I have hardened my frame against it. I have discovered God, says Tukā; fear has left me.

3289

IF you call me, I will come when you speak; I shall look forward with delight to getting some sweetmeats from you. When you call me, I shall eat them up at once. Tukā says, O God, all my actions are in your presence.

3290

THE end of life is sweetened by thee, so on thee I fix my affection. I shall pay no heed to pains and pleasures; they are the body's heavy lot; but within the body I shall make a dwelling-place for thee. Thy strength will set us free from toil and desire; we need not multiply our cares. Tukā says, *Now* we are crushed by their weight; but with you, of a surety, there is power divine.

3291

YOU are no wolfish mother, like other mothers of the world, that we should fear our words will be wasted, like chaff that bears no fruit. Thou art not weak, though thou hast no possessions. Thou art not false, says Tukā nor in any way an abject wretch.

3292

THE story of God I cannot do without; but in worldly life I only pretend to take a part. Your own mother is the best of mothers to *you*, whatever she is like; as for other mothers, if you like to honour them, you may do so. She who gave us birth yearns over us; her spirit is exceeding tender towards us. Tukā says, I pass my days in fond admiration for her, relying on her to support me.

3293

O INFINITE ONE, all I have to guide me is such guidance as thou vouchsafest. I shall not cease to fall at thy feet; what is in my heart will come forth from my lips. What I love is unalloyed faith; this will be sweet in the latter end. Tukā says, I shall not fail to observe the rules appointed me.

3294

WHERE you send me, I shall sing your praises; I shall give no thought to the aims of the body. So what I ask for is this sweetness in my throat; then everything that bars my way will perish. While I feel thy gracious glance upon me, I shall not fear the Kali age, though in future it grow in strength and power. Tukā says, I shall wave my flag at thy feet; thy name shall be easy for the world to attain.

3295

SEE how I have fixed all my thoughts on one aim; I have begun to suppress desire. My soul delights in nothing but thee; this is what I have vowed, O God! Though I know not thy secret, nothing shall interrupt my course; what I have worshipped, I shall still rejoice to worship. Tukā says, I have found that thy name is life; I listen to no news of other things.

3296

A MOTHER'S anger and her love exist side by side in her; but she is careful to remember the difference between them. Her irritation passes in a moment when it arises; her love never ceases. She knows how to teach lessons that make life sweet; assuredly, nothing interrupts her love. Before the due time comes, what she says is make-believe; but she knows when the time does come, and gives her child what is best for it. She makes no promises on his behalf, and lets no one torment him; though she frightens her own baby by telling him there's a snake coming. Tukā says, She takes good care of her children's life; she trembles for them and draws them to her side.

3297

WE are met in a close embrace, body to body; we are twined in each others arms. The service is mine, the kindness thine, O God! says Tukā.

3298

TRUTH is measured out more liberally; the currency of falsehood is circumscribed. It is known what will satisfy the test; this coinage is current everywhere. A ruler is not recognized while he stays at home; he must be set on the throne and honoured. Tukā says, What is true in itself will be recognized as true when it is reflected in a mirror.

3299

THERE is no gulf between you and me, O Viṭṭhala! How indeed could there be any wrongdoing on either side, when we have the four to do justice between us? I have found now the original written contract; I need not argue the point, says Tukā; my course is easy.

3300

WHY should I spare my body now? It is a paid retainer who will depart. Tukā says, I have opened up my mind; I am a plain, simple, generous man.

3301

NOW, I have only my father and mother in the world; there are no wicked men left to injure me. Why then, in respect of this matter, should the saints feel any anxiety about me? I am entrusted to the care of him who cherishes the universe; by his controlling power, he keeps the world in motion. Tukā says, O Pānduranga, it is thou who dost feed and cherish me.

3302

A CHILD petitioning is never hopeless; his mother is never unconcerned about him. Why should I be so impatient in my soul? The Lord of the senses knows my case. If sometimes he keeps me waiting, it is all in sport; there is no want of mercy in him. Tukā says, He knows what is best for us; no doubt he has ordained our lot.

3303

PERCHANCE, he has determined to amuse himself with me; he hungers for adoration, he sets us weeping. The mother hides herself and mystifies the child; but she is never so cruel as to leave him. Tukā says, She makes strange sounds to frighten her baby, and then she caresses him.

3304

TELL me, which of my thoughts is unknown to thee? Why need I form designs of my own? In this matter, thy authority prevails as thou hast established it; to testify to this, my voice proclaims thy commandment. When love is once born, no bodily embrace is needed; by inner contemplation its hue is deepened. Tukā says, What I have said up till now is nonsense; now I have firmly fixed my faith on thee.

3305

HOW can we take our fill of our parents' love? Of such a thing, how can it be possible to have enough? What is appointed will come to pass in its own due time; if a man tries to get his way by force, all that is left him is his own obstinacy. Only once, and briefly, need we make known our desires to him; all keys are in the hand of the Highest. Tukā says, The secret of secrets I have declared; now all careful thought is left to you.

3306

SLOWLY and comfortably, by easy stages, I have finished this journey. I have followed a road where children and cowherds journey together—the straight and level road of service to thee. Though we should feel weary, we must not deviate from this way. Tukā says, God is ever near his servants.

3307

MY wanderings in search of alms have met with success, a success proportioned to the distance I have travelled. I will sojourn here, and return home bearing with me a sign that I have reached my goal. Tukā says, The service of thy feet is gain which my eager desire has attained.

3308

MY mind has done well to start on this path; we can go home without fear, through the valour of this king of gods. We feel no need of other means of attainment; the praise of God fully proclaimed is all we need. Tukā says, His authority is supreme; who can stand in our way?

3309

IN him alone I trust; all other names to me signify nothing.

3310

I WILL sing to thee as best I may, careless strains or well-composed, with such skill as I possess. Tukā says, I do not feel it wrong; I am thy lisping child.

3311

WHAT pleasure can I feel in my lord's love, if it be a matter that embarrasses him? I will not ask thee, O Nārāyana, for anything that pains thee.

3312

WHEN I meet thee, I will tell thee the secret of my love; together, we will eat a sweet meal of joy. This is how a mother and her child behave.

3313

TUKĀ says, Entrust me to him in this way, then surely he will protect me.

3314

THOUGH many strangers may try to interest a child, yet, in his heart, he is only fond of his mother. He does not care to hear other men talking; he dances with delight when he sees her.

3315

WHATSOEVER wishes arise within me, take thou, O Nārāyana, the place of them. What particular wish need I distinctly state? Thou knowest every aspect of the mind. What other friend have I than thee, to whom I may tell my desires? The whole world has turned slanderous towards me; I cannot recall who are my friends or my enemies. Thou art the soul of our souls; my peace rests with thee, says Tukā.

3316

WITHOUT this gift from thee, says Tukā, I will not live; I had rather be a man demented.

3317

BEING limbs of thy body, we know thee completely; others find thee a riddle hard to penetrate. Thieves familiar with a house know where to lurk and whence to attack it. Tukā says, I have pierced a way in, and I come to talk to you.

3318

HE is generous in distributing his love; he considers not if a man is great or small. Sin has lost its power and retreated; Time has fled into exile.

3319

TEST my mind with all severity; my heart will not swerve from you. I will not lose my head for you; you shall see if I am miserly or generous. Crush me with a sledge-hammer; yet I shall not quit thy feet. Tukā says, as his last word, I cannot move forward without thee.

3320

THE giver is the consort of Lakshmī; how small is the boon I ask! He knows the thirst of the thirsty; but you cannot lessen the Ganges by brinking it. If it is the wishing-tree that is the giver, what will it cost it to satisfy one hungry man? Tukā says, By ceaseless contemplation, we have got hold of the highest Brahma.

3321

WHAT purpose stands unaccomplished through thy reserve, that I should trouble thee with force? My life is not passing away; I am suffering no loss; this I can easily recall I have no anxious cares; I am not dying of hunger, nor do I stand in need of buffaloes and kine. This you know full well; my words are long and tedious, but my faith is real. Tukā says, To gain perishable things mankind abandon your feet.

3322

WE have made God our debtor; what harm will it do us if we ignore other gods? Let us lay our entreaties before one alone; it is no use crying to others. If we cringe before many with troublesome requests, the end will not be purification. After full consideration, we have left all others alone. Tukā says, Let my faith repose at the feet of God; my soul will be gladdened.

3323

IF I cannot fill my belly with food, I will eat dust; but I will not lay a burden on thee. Priceless is thy name; Bramha and the rest know this not. Tukā says, True is thy name; it suffices by the impression it makes on men.

3324

I SHALL not look upon your face lest I should cast an evil eye on you; better far, I should first look on your feet. This body I shall give you to be waved round you and thrown away.

3325

WHAT entangled us, O God, in days gone by, that the rest of our lives should be filled with fears? Your fame in the world is still what it ever was; what is there that you ought to give us when you meet us? Some there are who sit fasting, to compel a gift from thee; there is no such obstinate persistence in us. The eagerness of these men brought disgrace on you; but what is there that *we* stand in need of? We desire not liberation nor dwelling-place in Vaikuṇṭha; we shall surrender our personal selves to thee. Tukā says, O Infinite One, if there is anything of mine you wish to have, take all that is mine!

3326

A GOPI went alone into a forest without the knowledge of her household. There was no one with her; she was unconcerned for her safety. When she had entered the impenetrable forest, she was beset by beasts of prey. She saw no path before her; an appalling fear came over her. Those whom she had left behind were far from her; there were obstacles ahead of her. Then, says Tukā, she began to think upon him who dwells in the heart.

XIV

The Moral Ideal

I—Purity from desire and passion

3327

HE on whom the wealth and wife of another make no impression, he is not, even in other directions, bound for a moment by the chain of actions. This experience is attained by the trusting soul; it sees the innermost truth laid bare before it. Search out this conclusion, that all fermented food is strong drink; though people have distinguished degrees of poison, and called some pure and some impure. Tukā says, Experience will show you what is really right in this matter; how can you buy your advantage with money?

3328

HUNGER goes no further than the stomach; it is desire that makes us fill our bag and brings shame on us; it is craving that increases our load. For indigestion, there are known remedies—unguents and cauterization; one who shaved his head or chin for it would be doing wrong. What is not prescribed is injurious, because you mistake its due application. The prescribed remedy must be applied in due measure, so far as the purpose requires. The man who avoids pollution, he is free from immorality. True service is obedience and fear; by this, says Tukā, you can preserve the wealth you have acquired.

3329

FIRST and foremost is renunciation of desire, then regard for such ordinances as concern one. One should view the body with indifference. Tukā says, Away with fear! Look dispassionately on the congenial and uncongenial.

11.—Sincerity

3330

BURN up all pretences, if there is aught wanting within! We may call bad good, but the end in view is still far from us. By haste you will do harm, if you take delight in haste. Tukā says, This shows you have no patience; your thoughts are not steady.

3331

SINCERITY alone passes muster with us; we look on everything else as waste of labour. Who would value pleasant speeches as long as he cannot make out the mind of him who utters them? Tukā says, All our troubles arise from knowledge; we ought not even to look on this evil creature.

3332

WHEN seed falls on deep, moist soil, it bears an excellent crop; the labour spent on shallow soil is wasted. We will not barter anything for false goods; that will only waste the store in our own bundle. Who is satisfied with a fine show in this world, a false exterior coupled with a real desire for a bellyful? Tukā says, That which will pass the test of fire, that alone will pass muster here—the genuine article.

3333

WHEN contentment is part of the mind's own nature, the mind is at peace; it can never turn back again to the world. Scrutinize articles to see if they are genuine, and you will be safe against loss. The false article can be distinguished; in lustre, it is far from the true. Tukā says, I prefer the true; so I am not in a hurry to make my choice.

3334

THE shell of the cocoanut is hard, but the inside is excellent. In accordance with this, remember, that purity inside is what we aim at. The jack-fruit has a thorny rind, but it is sweet within. The sugar-cane is hard and black without, but it is well-flavoured within. Our food owes its flavour to salt. Tukā says, The value of a thing depends on its inner qualities; what do its faults outside matter?

3335

A COPPER coin cannot compete with a coin of real value, though you may carry it all round the country. Wise men approve of nothing artificial; they like to see a thing approved by the elders. A crystal may look like a diamond, but a jeweller will not cast a glance at it. You may work up a piece of glass into a pearl, but a jeweller will not handle it. Tukā says, What is the use of a coquette's finery? Your own mind will tell itself what it thinks of it.

3336

TEST yourself, keep your aim unimpaired; an ornament purified in the fire receives additional lustre. You need converse with no one; view the world without concern; your mind will find repose. A man may deny that he has broken his fast, but a belch will disclose the truth; the liar's lie brings trouble on himself. Tukā says, The praise and blame of others are both idle; it is your own attitude of mind that bears fruit.

3337

AS long as a man has not subdued his senses, what is the use of his crying 'Rāma'? When food is tainted by a fly, it is not pleasant to eat it. If a man is to preach, his acts should correspond to what he sets forth. If such proof is not to be found in him, his preaching is no better than a song sung by a whore's handmaid. Tukā says, The saints will not let worldly passions contaminate them.

3338

A MAN who tells tales of battles, but has never met a foe in the field, when he sees other men carrying burdens, his heart begins to quake. But a man of generous temper, a king's warrior, he strikes with his sword. Blessed are his father and mother; penitence is born in him when he hears Hari's name. Tukā says, The words of the saints are sword-blades; they pierce the hearts of the wicked.

3339

IF a man acts as he speaks, I will salute his feet; I will be his servant and sweep his courtyard myself. I will wait on him with folded hands; he is a god, says Tukā; I lay my faith at his feet.

III.—Truthfulness

3340

NOT even God can set you free, so long as you are moaning beneath imaginary blows. Why do you not purify your idea of truth? your intellect is wasted, and you are whirled round in error. What room is there for setting up yourself, seeing that man is scattered among the five elements? Tukā says, You groan under a load, because you think the false true.

IV.—Humility

3341

OUR peace is thy feet, O Consort of Kamalā! I bow down, I roll on the ground before them. These alone I know, body, speech, and mind. I am humble among the people, says Tukā; I am lowest on the steps that lead to thee.

3342

THE penitent man—he who has forgotten his pride at the words of the ancient sages—let him set his feet on my forehead; it will be a time of blessing when I eat the food left by him. They who have spurned the six passions—who rush to seek the Saints' protection—Tukā says, Their very nature will be changed; they will be pure at heart even in their own homes.

3343

THE man who stands up for a public disputation will be caught by some opponent's trick. How can the reed possess any strength of its own? It makes the water its ally. A violent man finds his peer in strength; while a humble man makes himself free from oppression. Tukā says, That which enters into union with all liquids finds an ally in all of them.

3344

I DESIRE not the gift of sweet utterance; let a growing faith dwell in my mind. Do not let your life be parted from Nārāyana; then, though you have not knowledge, you may very well be stupid. The best lot in life for you is one which men dispraise; the burden of dignity is useless. Tukā says, Let there be a settled faith in your soul—mercy, kindness, and peace with all creatures.

V.—Peacefulness

3345

IF you greet men with the words 'A blessing on you', all sense of hostility vanishes. Nārāyana has fully assured us of this, by the sense of love he has planted in our hearts. These words put to flight all anxious care. Tukā says, If you sing this song, your own advantage comes forward to meet you.

3346

'HATE none; be jealous of no being'; this is our principle. Tukā says, Follow this principle and you will be free from blame; we offer you teaching which will benefit you.

VI.—Perseverance

3347

WITH so much gained, should loss result, whom will you blame in the end? The valiant man bears every blow that falls on him; when once he has advanced his foot, he does not draw it back. His danger I compare to the obstacles that threaten us when we stray from the feet of Govinda. The battle-field of life is a critical place, says Tukā; results will be proportioned to the efforts you put forth.

3348

WHOSO stands on the shore of a stream he must cross, he should not leap into the water. He should adopt the same measures as those who went before him; he should not think they look too easy. Moreover, says Tukā, the onslaught of idleness often ruins a man.

3349

WE decide if a dinner is a good one by the last morsel; the same rule holds in every case. You must not change your mind till the very last, or all the trouble you have taken will be wasted. If you have assumed a part, you must carry it through; you will be ridiculed if you fall short in it. Tukā says, If a man begins cooking, without knowing the secrets of the art, his intelligence will suffer a slur.

3350

A MAN imposes on himself a hasty impulse towards faith; but this is waste of effort and a hindrance to steadiness. Let a man, therefore, weigh carefully his proceedings; that speech is wise which leaves something unsaid. Idle talk about renunciation is ostentatious pride; true courage is shown in endurance; it is part of a man's nature. Tukā says, The right thing is a fountain that wells up continually; what use is a mere pool where water collects?

VII.—The service of others

3351

If a man rejoices over the misfortunes of others, his pleasure and their pain and his censure too recoil on himself. Harbour not such thoughts in your mind; do not store up for yourself a capital of sin. This will linger in your mind as a torment and affliction; it will cast it into fire, till its place of rest is burned up. Tukā says, Thus all your merits will be destroyed; what is destined for us, the operation of our past brings to pass.

VIII.—General

3352

If we dash our head against a rock we shall break it, but the rock will not sweat in sympathy with the pain it causes us. A man may rashly adventure himself near a live coal, but what pleasure will he have in grasping it? Tukā says, If a man is sullen towards us, we look on his silence as we look on that of the sky.

3352 a

OUR childhood lasted twelve years; that was wasted in ignorance; thus our life passed vainly away; we served not the Lord of Pānḍhari. There were left eighty-eight years, thirty of which were spent in lustful desires. Thus fifty-eight were left; of these, thirty were spent in fond affection. Thus twenty-eight were left, wherein we forgot body and home. Tukā says, This is clear account; our worldly life is but a span.

3352 b

IF the she-ass be in milk, can she compare with the cow? Hang garlands round the neck of a crow,—will he thereby assume the grace of a *hansa*. Wash an ape, and set the *tila* upon him, can he go through the actions of a Bramhāna? Should a Bramhāna lose all his attributes, still, says Tukā, he is supreme in the three worlds.

3353

THUS did a tiger seek to persuade a jackal, "Let me eat you up comfortably. You must infallibly die some day; why should you starve me to death?" "Excellent" replied the other "You have settled the proper course yourself. *You* are bound to perish; if you let me off, you will have a good deed to your credit." "Oh! but this is what you ought to consider," says the other. When one rogue meets another, this is how they naturally talk, says Tukā.

3354

WE should give food to all creatures, but money only after due consideration of their fitness; for we should only sow seed where it will grow. Otherwise, while intending to do well, we may sin, like one who should fatten a snake on milk, or purchase sorrow for himself by reciting weird spells. The earth is all the same to look at; nevertheless, parts of the soil are rocky, parts gravelly, and parts of black earth. Some are good, some poor, and some middling. Hence, if you wish to do right, you must first discriminate. Tukā says, A choice dish prepared without sugar would have no flavour.

3355

I WILL tell you exactly how many houses there were in Lanka; five lakhs of stone, and seven of brick; of bell-metal and copper, one crore; of pure gold, seven crores. Yet, says Tukā, he who owned all this wealth took not one cowri to heaven with him.

3356

WE need not court food or sleep; they are ready to greet us themselves. Speech not measured to the occasion is futile; much or little, it is a weariness to the flesh. He alone knows self-content who knows when he has had enough by signs within him. Tukā says, Do nothing which will distress you; then you may live as you please.

3357

CLOSE up every path of wandering; enter no devious side-path in the jungle.

3358

A MAN cannot change his nature to save his life; what is in him comes to the surface. The same disposition pervades him within and without; he never grows tired of his own sentiments or gives them up. If you strike a diamond with a hammer, it enters the substance of the hammer; it cannot renounce its own enduring hardness. Tukā says, It is the nature of sandal to burn itself and make others cool.

3359

IF you separate the cow from the calf, each is moved by the comfort they feel in each other. We remark the persistent folly of the man who separates them, for each pines after the other, Hunger longs for food; in fact, food was created to provide for hunger. Tukā says, Things move according to the disposition they feel towards each other.

3359 a

A MAN'S likings make themselves known; his nature shows itself by outward signs. The thoughts of the heart come to the lips; attention assists the mind. The longings of the pregnant woman affect the unborn child; a light is reflected from a polished dish. Tukā says, We should take the course we think proper; we should eat what we think we ought to eat.

3360

WHEN food has once been cooked, if you kindle fuel, it is wasted. Avoid, then, needless toil; all excess is futile. Cherish this secret truth,--that duty consists in doing what fits the occasion. Tukā says, You will comprehend this when the time for action comes.

3361

IF the vine be of nectar, the fruits are of nectar, and the seed afterwards will be of the same strain. Grant me, O Nārāyaṇa, to dwell with men whose words are like nourishing moisture. The best of food is that which comforts the throat, and shows itself in the sleekness and lustre of the body. Tukā says, We become like those we live with; the odour of sandalwood cleaves even to man's body.

3362

WHEN you see good men before you, let your speech be without reproach; this is righteousness; you will gain nothing here by passion. Self-restraint is called for; a wise man will recognize the occasion. Tukā says, Much the best thing is meekness.

3363

THE only man who can do a thing really well is the man on whose head that burden is placed. Those who went before and those who follow are alike unequal to the task; experience shows this. Within the magic stone is infinite gold; but a base metal is all base within. A man does his own allotted duty; this secret, Tukā knows.

3364

WHEN the mind lights on what it likes, it is soothed and pacified. When the mind delights in goodness, Nārāyana is not displeased.

3365

LIKE a diamond shattered by the touch of a bug's blood, such is a holy man ruined by evil company. Even a good cow is ruined by the company of an unruly one; a moment is enough to change her. Base metal will render gold impure, so that its value disappears by lakhs and crores. Sweet dishes turn bitter if you poison them; such is the effect of bad company on men. Tukā says, with full assurance, Good company is the best; bad company will keep you in the cycle of the eighty-four.

3366

THE monkey knows the cocoanut by its outer rind alone; but one who eats it takes off its covering. One drinks the juice, another's mouth is filled with earth; they have each his own portion assigned them. If you give milk and rice to a dog, he vomits them up; but they will nourish amply one who can enjoy them. Tukā says, Fools bear the load; wise men carry away the essence.

3367

SHOULD I be beaten by mankind, I would set myself far from the world; then, in my misery, I would slowly remember God. Should dishonour overtake me, should misfortune, 'twould be well. The best thing that can happen to us, says Tukā, is that our dignity should perish.

3368

THE contented in spirit will join with me; they will come when they hear my call; they will say, We two are one. Tukā says, In our speech, they perceive the marks of Viṭṭhala.

3369

OUR parents do not know what is best for us; they teach us the rules of worldly conduct. If a blind man grasps a blind man's stick, both leader and follower will come to grief at once. We must not step ahead too hastily; deliberation is needed; it is the bait on the hook which sticks in the fish's throat. Tukā says, The horse and his rider come at once to a decision which is to be master.

3370

STONE images for religion, golden slippers to wear, these the rich may possess; if a man of no name carries a rich man's seal, people will recognize it, though they may think little of him. Tukā says, Those persistent claims are a mistake; each should take refuge in his lot.

3371

THOSE who wield the weapon of forgiveness —what can the wicked do to them? If a forest fire breaks out where there is no grass, it must die out of its own accord. Tukā says, Forgiveness benefits all mankind; practice it continually, and make yourselves happy.

3372

TO revile any one is sinful; to grieve any man is to grieve God. Therefore I have diligently taught my mind to think of God and nothing else. Even though we set our tongue in motion to serve other men, still, the sinful taint of the world clings to it. Tukā says, Our souls are subject to their past; who will save us from distress? What gladdens our eyes is pity.

3373

WE delight in the company of a man whose mind harmonises with ours; if a man irritates us, it is best to keep away from him. This view has come down to us from many generations; every one makes it a rule to leave undesirable people alone. We should never associate with people whose nature is different from our own, be it father, son, relative, or any one else. Tukā says, This true maxim we should observe; we should not do otherwise.

3374

THOUGH a man may not have tasted food for seven days, still, he should not neglect a preaching. Though our head be broken and our body cut to pieces, still, we should not cease to shout aloud his name. Tukā says, If a man is thus resolved concerning God's name, God dwells with him for ever.

IX.—Freedom from the sense of self

3375

IT is the sense of self which divides us from him and ruins us; it is this which, in this world, pollutes us. He whom it touches not, he is blest; he is a light to lighten his family. This sense of self is self-slaughter; it keeps us from attaining the truth. Tukā says, It leads a man to hold his head high and keep on complaining.

3376

IF two friends are equally rich, they treat each other as equals; there is peace in one spot between them. When, however, there is no spring of sympathy in their hearts, but only artificial courtesy on each side, friendship is like a pool of stagnant water which may vanish. The magic stone changes the nature of iron, as the wise change the nature of fools; but the change is only one in name, the stone remains a stone. Tukā says, As long as there is not a spirit in men that recognizes their two souls as one, nothing passes between them but idle amusement.

X.—Be impartial to all men

3377

KNOW that the whole earth is pure; what is impure is desire. Thus people are vexed without cause, and give up the fray before they are wounded. All men are gods; it is base doubt that strips them. Tukā says, When we banish this sense of difference, then all are pure.

3378

I LOOK on all men as gods, thus I have forgotten my own faults and virtues. The image in the mirror seems distinct from the object, but it is really the same with it. Tukā says, When the stream meets the sea, it loses its own water.

3379

HOW can the pure and the impure be sorted out, when even the skin and flesh of men cannot be separated? With God, no quality makes a thing great or small. Is water a different thing according as it comes from a stream, a well, a rivulet, or a river? Does the sun choose out rays for different purposes? His splendour sucks up all moisture alike. The milk of different cows does not vary in colour; it is the same in the case of all. You cannot distinguish between different kinds of earth, but pots have different names according as they are prepared in different ways. Fire behaves always in the same way; it does not consider one sort of fuel pure and another impure. Tukā says, The fitness of the receiver is the point we should consider;—or shall we say that nectar is sweet if it is mixed with poison?

3380

TRUE worship of all is to cherish all creatures; envy of others brings weariness with it. Let the object of our resentment and irritation be ourselves; then the rest of the world we shall look on as Hari. This, says Tukā, is to be truly a saint—to identify our own soul with the souls of all men.

3381

MILK yields curds, butter, and ghee; so, likewise, all visible creatures are united by a common nature. Behold, various ornaments are made of gold; but they share in the common nature of gold. Various vessels are moulded out of clay; but as clay they are all identical. Tukā says, The same One is one and many; unity pervades multiplicity.

XI.—Compassion

3382

WERE an enemy to offer you his neck, you should spare him; you should protect a suppliant at the risk of your own life. Men of power swear by reason alone; let the good, therefore reason out when is right and wrong. Tukā says, By preserving his good name, honour, and success, does a man attain to God.

XV

Life under the influence of Religion

3383

ALL my anxious cares are with Viṭṭhoba; if I forget him for a moment, I lose a profit worth many lakhs. The feet of my Viṭṭhoba within my heart are like the plant that revives the dead.

3383 a

OUR natural bent is to simple faith; the splendours of dialectic can never find a place with us. The mother knows all her child's ways; she never lets it irritate her; she puts it to her breast. O Merciful One! *You* may assume any shape; but I must not let anything pollute my mind; I must not take pleasure in anything save thy worship. Let me dream of thy form, and utter thy name with my lips, says Tukā, whether my eyes are set on men, or on things liquid or solid.

3383 b

THAT my spirit was reborn within his spirit, this is the doing of my master. If he bestows the gift of his favour upon me, then I shall see his wondrous work. If a fearless spirit is implanted in me, his orders I shall obey. To spread devotion abroad, we employ the services of bards. For our success, our master must answer; the servants need do nothing but serve. Tukā says, To one as persistent as I am, some answer should be vouchsafed.

3384

WHEAT can be prepared in many forms; the tongue dances through the pleasure they give. Though the dish be finished, yet pleasure in it reappears, as the sea shows us waves following each other. The mother never forgets her child; though once she has suckled it, she suckles it again and again. Tuka says, Some sweet juice is left in the mouth, and we taste it again and again.

3385

SUCH as sincerely offer themselves to God, and humble themselves before all mankind, they are masters of all glory. God will not suffer them to break away from himself; yet, so strong is their devotion, that they keep a place of their own. Whether with their knowledge or without it, this state has passed over them, so God accommodates himself to their desire. Tukā says, Better far is the life of the child, for the mother nourishes him at her breast.

3386

THE name of Hari has spread abroad like a creeper; it is loaded with fruits and flowers. Perch on it, O my soul, like the prince of birds, to accomplish thy full satisfaction. The original seed foretold the sweetness which was soon to be realized. Tukā says, Time fleets by moment after moment; that sweet savour will pass away.

3387

TUKĀ says, I have suffered no obstacle to keep me back; I have suffered no delay.

3388

COME, let us vanquish this Kali age; it is feeble in comparison with our strength. Let us take our fill of passion, revel, frolic, laughter, and mirth. Twist your necks, if you will, and chatter nonsense; Nārāyana loves that every one should please himself. Dance, therefore, as ye will before each other; here, there is neither great, nor small, nor lowly. Tukā says, Let no one interrupt the course of love; to distinguish God from his worshippers would be a sin.

3389

MY mind has grown sick of the world.

3390

THROUGH love for his attributes, I lengthen out my speech; I have forgotten everything else. From beginning to end, there is nothing to part us; soul is merged in soul. Tukā says, My body is rendered altogether cool, by this joy of Bramha.

3391

BY constraining speech, I have laid hold of Bramha; I have put away every other effort. Name and form have been tied up in a bundle, and we have got rid of them all at once. Tukā says, All delay on the road has been ended; deliverance has been put into our hands.

3392

BIRTH, possessions, lineage, they enjoy the advantage of all these who have Nārāyana stored up in the vessel of the heart. There is neither rising nor setting to their lustre, says Tukā.

3393

THE mind plays and hovers round your feet, imagining it is doing right; at last it settles on them. No false dealings are any use here, for thou knowest the heart, O Pānduranga! We have made Time to be as though it were not, by handing over to thee our pains and pleasures.

3394

MY desires have been realized in this, that Hari's name has come to my lips. Let us feed on it now to our heart's content, so that nothing will be left behind. We have as much as we want stored up. Tukā says, These three letters, Viṭṭhala, have brought this to pass.

3395

I HAVE seen the whole world as Viṭṭhala; this has soothed my frame.

3396

GOD has given me a place where I need not die, a place in his own house, where I have ample room. Tukā says, Now we dwell together; 'mine' and 'thine' have vanished.

3397

THIS speech that I utter, these flowers of words, let them lie at last on thy feet. I have bidden farewell to the body, and given up all consciousness of it; I have banished all difference between my soul and the soul of God. I have laid my soul at thy feet, says Tukā; fulfil my earnest petition!

3398

THE exchange has now taken place; why should we consider which of us is larger or smaller? We have fallen into each others hands, so now we are both free from care. Neither of us can draw back now, since all has taken place before witnesses. Tukā says, What room is there left for desire?

3399

I HAVE surrendered my sense of self to you, I have given up my own place in the world; I am now entirely under your control. I have killed myself, and you have established yourself in me. Tukā says, Neither 'I' nor 'mine' exists here now.

3400

As pure as is the Ganges stream, so pure is the portion in our cooking-pot. We like our meal better at each mouthful, when we are feeding on the juice of Bramha. With such choice dishes before us, we delight in them, even when we are satisfied. Tukā says, When the mind is pure, it enjoys Nārāyana.

3401

HOW handsome we look when we are singing Hari's praises! Yet we wear neither dress nor jewels; we have the world for our servant. This, says Tukā, is the effect of thy service, O Hari.

3402

WE feel disposed to eat what we have been used to eating; we meet with loving joy a friend whom once we met. We never weary of Pāndu-ranga; our longing for him grows upon us. The desire of our senses to behold him may be satisfied and stilled; but the mind continues for ever to meditate on him. Tukā says, We fill our stomachs, but we are hungry still.

3403

WHEN we truly remember God all fear departs from us. We need not be anxious; he has power to control all things. Our faith dwells steadfastly at his feet; when this is so, God is near us. Tukā says, As we utter Kṛishṇa's name, a peaceful love to all men is born within us.

3404

HOW did we grow so fond of him? It has brought many quarrels on us. Men like me, the world says, are mad after God. He has come forth from solitude; though he be veiled, he cannot be hidden from us. Tukā says, When we meet him, we are severed from ourselves.

3405

PĀNDURANGA has showed me no favour; I fill my belly along with the saints. When men of skill are gathered together, the learned and the talented assemble; I am but a feeble slave of Vishṇu. Tukā says, I know not how to satisfy objectors; I hold fast the feet of Viṭṭhobā.

3406

I AM amused to hear my mind and my soul conversing together of their joy and delight in the Spotless One. When we have well digested our food, we retaste the flavour of it from time to time; the pleasure it gives us increases our desire for it. The bliss of solitude has penetrated my soul; I have grown sick of the world. My intelligence will never again be fit for the world; I have addicted myself to your feet, O Govinda. Tukā says, This is my settled conviction; my mind has found repose in Pānduranga.

3407

THROUGH the controlling power of our master, the secret is first placed in our hands; as we advance, the greater and greater is our gain. I utter fond and foolish words, but they come moist from the very core of my being; a father and mother love the endearing prattle of their child. My mind mingles with his; I am truly wise, not by repute alone. I have brought to the surface the signs of his grace within me. I am not wearied by length of time; I have watched every moment with wakeful care; Tukā will not leave God for one moment.

3408

BY churning, we bring forth for use the essence of milk; but even those who get the butter-milk are glad of it. Sweet is the fruit of toil; experience teaches men how delightful it is. Cooking and well-flavoured food—how can we expect to find these everywhere? Tukā serves out such food to the row of saints; he loves to associate with them.

3409

NIGHT is vanished; I do not see how sleep can ever overpower me now. I have built my home in Nārāyana; I shall enjoy eternal joy. I have fenced the place round; I have cleared it of this idle 'my' and 'mine'. Let us live together, says Tukā; we shall not be parted for a moment.

3410

MY mouth revels in this juice of love ; it delights in it hugely. Tukā says, Viṭṭhala is a measure true and ample, sufficient for our needs.

3411

MY feet have travelled along this path ; in the feet of the saints, I have beheld him. My sins are destroyed; poverty has harried them to death ; at the same time, too, it has purified my body. Tukā says, All my concerns have ended well ; my rebirth has borne fruit.

3412

WHEN you see faith in me, you will take steps to ensure my welfare. I feel neither pleasure nor pain nor anxiety about such things ; this is still my mood, whatever desires may cross my mind. Do thou break these fetters from off me, without imposing any toil on me. Tukā says, I am free from care ; I have embraced the bliss of solitude with Pānduranga.

3413

WHAT need the suppliants care for birth or death ? On their lips is the life-giving name, O Bearer of the Disc ! In their hearts is reflected thy shape fully out-lined ; how can the world extend its limits there ? Tukā says, Under the shelter of thy feet, we can trample down the Kali age.

3414

RENUNCIATION and pleasure we unite, when we sing of Pānduranga ; we repel the assault of the senses. Once for all we repose ; the mind is restless no more ; Vithala takes all our burden upon him. Like a mother-bird, he brings us food in his bill and claws ; he brings it home to us, and puts it in his children's mouths. Tukā says, Through this love of his, we have sunk ourselves in the sea of his feet ; the treasure of our births in the past, all that we have gained, is there.

3415

WE shall eat this meal ready-prepared for us ; there are no hills we need climb ; this will open up still further our trade in happiness. We have gotten for an inheritance our place at thy feet ; no stranger can encroach on it. We have sacrificed our souls for it ; we have forgotten the very name of everything else. We have embraced a faith in One alone ; our assurance has borne fruit. Tukā says, We have grown to be sturdy fellows ; we have a place very close to thee ; do thou make good now the words we have uttered.

3416

WE are free from fear, where there is no cause for repentance in the soul. Where there is an eager desire for God, what taint can make that heart impure ? As soon as you confess your sin, he lets not a particle of it remain. Tukā says, Our souls are penetrated by his love.

3417

HOW can God be far from those that pray to him for compassion? A child petitioning need not cling to his mother; she knows what sweets to give him. If a man puts his weight into a boat, the farther shore is not far from him. Tukā has now left mankind; he is transported to another land.

3418

I SHALL no more suffer my mind to be divided; I shall not leave Viṭṭhobā's feet. I shall not let the wind of any other blow upon my body. I shall now come and go with God; this I have done since that day. What, have I lost all, that I should disquiet myself? There is Pānduranga, standing before and behind me. Tukā says, I ask for abounding love—for the fruits of Vaikunṭha to be enjoyed on earth.

3419

A LAMP-WICK gives forth a light when you light it; but a diamond shines naturally. Some accumulate wealth by great exertions; some have it presented to them by good fortune. The sandal-tree has fragrance as its characteristic; the man is an ass who tries to separate them. Tukā says, If a man bears the impress of Hari, he is not only saved, as a matter of course, but he is honoured by men.

3420

WE forgot that we exist; such is our state, that, in the body, we escape from the body. Tukā says, We have become like fire; we shall not let sin or merit touch us.

3421

MY faith is not like the labour of a man impressed; no unproductive means do I adopt. I do not merely attach thy form to my soul; my innermost desire is set on thee. As a miser counts his coppers, so I count my time by minutes and seconds. O Lord of the world, says Tukā, stand close by my side.

3422

THE man whom he takes for his associate he makes like himself; so, many a time, I have run to and from him. If a man is disposed to love him, he kindles love within him, and he entangles though he does not fetter him. Tukā says, In tales concerning thy name, we do sufficiently meet thee, O God!

XVI

Our Attitude towards the World

I.—The Problem

3423

WE dwell both with God and the world; we stand with loins girt up to pass from one scene to the other. We speak the language of both sides; our service gives us authority over our Lord. His command was revealed but once; we must act according to the rules he gave. Tukā says, I make obeisance to him, standing where I stood.

3424

THE body is a sweet placed in the way that leads to death; this much I have learned full easily. But this it is I ask in wonder—What have men found durable in it? The course of our past has made it a mere channel for divers experiences. Tukā says, We poor creatures cannot solve this riddle.

3425

LET us quaff this nectar, for we know of none other. Pleasure and pain, suffering and disease we must endure, according as they are reserved for us. What I aspire to, O God, says Tukā, is thy feet.

3426

WATER is steady where its bed is smooth, and unsteady where it is rough; a broken slope sets it roaring. The secret is easy, but people do not control their mind; the demon of error is deeply rooted in the mind. Water cannot break up the orb of the sun; imitate *him* and not his reflection. Tukā says, A man dreads a rope till the truth has penetrated his mind.

3427

'TIS thou, O Viṭṭhala, that art real; why then hast thou shown us this outward form of the world? Rein in and rule this illusion of thine! I cry aloud to thee; why hast thou stricken us thus with fear? Thou hast given a name to a thing that has truly no form; thou hast raised up empty solicitudes. Tukā says, What moved thee to show this subtlety, when thou wast free from all form, from all concern?

3428

THROUGH the evil destiny of man, this purpose entered into thee; now, though we purify ourselves, we cannot attain to thee. If this diversion of thine perished, what should we miss? As it is, thou hast set a difference between us and thee. Show me where sin and merit exist in embodied forms; why dost thou lead us to dream they exist? Now, says Tukā, away with this jugglery; it is a groundless torment, O Pānduranga.

3429

OUR parents did not know our true interests; they instructed us in the ways of the world. We are like a blind man grasping the stick of a blind man in front of him; they will perish both of them together, in front and rear. We should not follow the ways of men; we should give the case due consideration; the bait at the end of the line brings the fish to the hook. Tukā says, I have made a decision swift and sure, separating at once the rider from his horse.

3430

THIS whole universe is a sport of thine; thou hast put it together with subtle skill. Thou hast set the spirit of self between us and thee; it stands as an obstacle before us and the world. Come before us as thou art in thyself; thou knowest how to show and how to hide thyself. How long, says Tukā, will thou torment us?

3431

I TEACH others to understand the words I learned myself; the mirrored image of a treasure is useless to others than the owner. How can I make real experience my own? This problem stands before me. I sing, I dance, I go through the postures prescribed for the body; but it is you who must give me the secret of the skill which leads to attainment. Tukā says, I cannot bear the delay you have made; if you will give it me, I am fully prepared for it.

3432

NOT the space of a seed is empty of thee in the whole world, so the world assures us. Ascetics, saints, and sages have declared thou art everywhere. Trusting to this, I sought thy protection; I am a creature of thine from ancient times. Thou pervadest all the worlds, and art yet left outside them; there is no place where I cannot find thee. 'There is no limit to my nature and therefore I cannot meet my worshippers'—Is such thy opinion, and hence thou comest not? O tell us, says Tukā, how to reach thy feet.

II.—That we should make the most of it

3433

IF 'mine' and 'thine' vanish, then this burden will be lightened. There will be nothing then to do or undo, for the world is naturally pure. It is desire and the snare of illusion that have put the halter on our necks. Be ready to honour pleasure when it comes; do not moan over sorrows. If you do but utter Nārāyana's name; if you count gain and loss the same, honour and dishonour, then, says Tukā, your life may truly be called pure.

3434

WHY should we lead abject lives? Our past brings us into the world; the right thing, then, is a steady spirit of courage. Whatever may betide us can be no great disaster. Tukā says, If God is merciful to us, all is well.

3435

I HAVE to undergo unremunerative bodily toil; I am not void of actions, like you. I will not spare anything now; I will employ all my powers to worship you. Not that I hope for anything from you; I am quite indifferent to my body's needs. Tukā says, My disquietude has vanished.

3436

THE body given us by God is excellent for his service; yet it has become a field fruitful in error and confusion. When a man stiffens and straightens his neck through self-conceit, there is no bending it. Such a man cannot frame his tongue to call himself a servant of God, but he opens wide his throat for wanton speech. Tukā says, Where shall I go to leave this filth behind me, and purify myself by ablution?

3437

WHEN we need sugar, we buy it at a grocer's shop; what concern have we with his caste or family? A tulsi-plant may spring upon a heap of refuse; why should we reject it because it grew in such a place? A cow feeds naturally on filth; is that any reason why we should not drink her milk? Tukā says, What have we to do with the rind of the jack-fruit? We should take out the seeds and eat them.

3438

GIVE up the sugar, but enjoy its sweetness; give up the salt, but enjoy its saltness. So give up the world, and thereby you will attain to God.

III.—That we should renounce it

3439

THE world is a foul place; the very sight of it is pollution. Our duty here is to show kindness to all creatures; this is the conclusion to which truth leads us. This is not merely my own opinion; I call in the saints to bear witness to it. Tukā says, Taught by experience, the soul will also avow the same.

3440

THE cause brings about its result; desire brings about weariness. What avails then such attachment? Eagerly let us contemplate Pāndu-ranga. Men beat their breast in passion for him, while yet they do not truly love his form; they are more and more enraptured with his outer shape, says Tukā.

3441

BY making void the world, we have brought into existence a course of duty ever broadening and full of merit. The worship of Hari has conferred lustre on the world; the assault of Kali has been repulsed. I need no means of approach now; I have done what was needed; I have given up all sense of the body. Tukā says, In the story of Hari is the bliss of mystic union; he who sings it knows naught of the misery of the world.

3443

GIVE me that contemplation of thee which destroys Time, which leads one away from wealth, honour, and the world. When the body dies we must leave behind bile, phlegm, and wind; while as yet all my members are active, I have once for all sent up this cry to thee. Thou, says Tukā, art the creator of all these; thou art also the hearer of all this.

3444

TO the disillusioned, the body is a thing of nought; they have no desire for anything. Tukā says, My longing is to approach thy feet.

3445

NEITHER father, mother, nor wealth can accompany you; you must suffer that which your store of merit brings to pass. Consider then what will really advantage you; do not attach yourself to the ways of the world. You will, some day, leave life behind you; there is no reality about the body. Tukā says, Time has taken in hand the measure; he is gathering up thy sin and merit.

3446

SIN means persistent attachment to the world; the *Yogi* must give up all desires. When such a treasure is so easy to come by, why do you waste words? What is there you may not compass, when you have the means to it in the mind itself? Take this comfortable path, says Tukā, and break the head of desire.

3447

I WAS far from thee while I cherished doubts of my own; I did not understand the true nature of the distinction between us. Now thou shalt be my companion everywhere; I shall not leave thee anywhere space to hide in. The illusive world made me late in coming to thee; hence this distance that was left between us. Tukā says, Why dost thou show thyself as separate from us? What a waste of labour is the game of hide-and-seek!

3448

TIME pursues me as though I were a sheep; this is his point of attack—the worthless notion of 'me' and 'mine'. I have carried on my head a burden of unreality; there is no reality in it when a man sees through it. Tukā says, I have brought near me what was far from me; it was the mirage that lay between us.

3449

IT is best if, from the first, you form no attachment to the world; it is death to the over-trustful, so they say. Think honestly what is best for me, O Pānduranga! I have no faith, but I call myself thy slave; why, says Tukā, dost thou find it wearisome to save the distressed?

3450

IF any one expresses a desire to you, you keep the petitioner far from you. I, therefore, have done away with all desires; it is desire that is the root of difference. Through thy love for me, there flows a stream of milk from thy breast. Tukā says, Speak out in answer to my prayer.

3451

AS I eat and drink at home, I meditate on his name at each mouthful; I keep awake from moment to moment, for I fear lest any other theme should enter my mind. I stand outside the courtesies of life, the proceedings in which men display their pride and love of honour. Tukā has grown wiser; he hides himself, for shelter, behind Nārāyana.

3452

THREATEN me not, O mind of mine; I have turned my back on the cares of the world. Whatever plans men form, though they be guiltless, lead to sin. They engender fear, they bring tribulation on the soul. Tukā says, Whatever happens, I will look on; I will dwell in peace.

3453

THIS is what I have gained, O Viṭṭhala—prostration of myself before thee; I speak of nothing else. Where do other things bring us any fruition? By fitting means, must ends be gained. Tukā says, We must burn up the impulses which crowd in upon us.

3454

VILE as I am, I am disgusted with this body of mine; it is quite enough for me that I have once more been associated with a thing of this kind. How often must I die in time to come? I cling to Viṭṭhobā. Who will honour this body now? Let shame fall on it. Tukā says, What I abandon, I will abandon for ever; who would be so cowardly as to turn back from this act.

3455

LET us store up virtues; let us not walk on any other path. Men crave various pleasures; they enter devious tracts and weary themselves. We, however, have the gathering of the saints appointed us to join. Tukā says, I look with astonishment on the way mankind amuse themselves.

3456

NĀRĀYANA loves unity; he is grieved by any estrangement from him; so we should not suffer the smallest change to pass over us. We should do away with all nonsense, and escape from the idle uproar of men; the true place of joy is solitude. Body, speech, and mind, if you devote yourselves to the contemplation of his primal form, you will reach it as swiftly as an arrow cleaves its mark. Tukā says, Set a stone on sloth and sleep; be persevering; know that only while embracing him are you awake.

3457

IN accumulating riches, you move further and further from God; you drift down the stream of life. There is nothing you need; faith alone will bring you to the goal. I swear by Viṭṭhala, says Tukā.

3458

YOU may heap up millions of riches, but not a rag leaves the world with you. You may chew betel-leaves beyond number, but your face will be wan when you depart. You may love beds and mattresses and cushions, but you will keep company at last with the cow-dung cakes. Tukā says, Rāma is our only refuge; if you forget him, you will suffer misery.

3459

THE story of a battle is pleasant in the ears, but to take part in one is agony. The worship of Hari is like a cake on a pole; the men who distinguishes himself by capturing it is a rare hero. If we fatten up the body, it becomes a henchman of pleasure; the lord of Vaikuṇṭha forsakes it. Tukā says, We ought to fling away the body, to gain the consort of Rakumini.

3460

STRIP the leaves from trees and eat them; remember Nārāyana incessantly. Wrap round your waist the bark of trees, and wear it; forget that you have a body. Think of men's praise as though it were food vomited up; live in solitude for Viṭṭhala's sake. Maintain no friendly bearing towards the world; dwell by yourself in the wilderness. Whoso makes this his resolve, says Tukā, his cravings will be cleared away.

3461

THROUGH his illusive manifestations, men are so deceived, that they fall into sin by various actions. Yet why should we love or honour the world? It is well to set it far from us.

Various passions and fancies dwell within us; even great ascetics have been severely tormented by them. Thus do I teach thee, says Tukā, O mind! Be thou ashamed henceforth.

3462

WOMEN, sons, and wives are part of the illusion of the world; none of them is a reality at the latter end. They hand us over bound to Yama; they strip the ornaments off our corpse. How can we trust thieves like these? We cling to your waist, says Tukā.

3463

WE should not form many projects in all sorts of directions. When a man is not head of a village or a district, if he takes on himself the office of a village-accountant—well, you need not go far to look for sin; if you want to see it, you will find it with *him*. Another man takes up the collection of tolls; sin is always at home with him. The sale of cows, buffaloes, and ghee—those who carry it on are rogues. Observe, says Tukā, There is no room for merit in these trades.

3464

THE projects we form are the sources of sin and merit. They originate in the mind; the mind conforms itself to the fancies that arise in it. When we refuse to do or not to do, to stir or to advance, *then* call us good. Tukā says, Our life may truly be called a sea.

3465

WORLDLY life and life with the highest—he who acts both parts together, in the end he achieves neither. If a man seeks to lay his hands on two grain-pits at once, he will end by destroying himself.

3466

THE ignorant seek for wealth through devotion; how can there be any true perception in their souls? The ignorant offer worship with their thoughts full of desire; how can they bring God before their minds? They perform rites with their thoughts set on gain; how can they find means of approach wherein are no selfish aims? Their knowledge is of objects sensuous; how can they attain to the eternal Bramha? Fie on their faces! says Tukā; they recruit the bandit-hordes of ignorance.

3467

WHAT of the million means of salvation? If we try them, they are labour lost. If God shows us his favour, this will add lustre to our form. Vain was all the trouble we took, as long as we did not relinquish the world. Tukā says, Now we know that every thing follows its own nature.

3468

IT is well now; I learned my lesson this very morning. Keep me no more upon this earth; a mistake was made when I came here. I knew not that the age before me would bring such consequences with it. Tukā says, Keep me, if you must, in this hell of a world, to finish my lot.

3469

IF you live with thieves, your mind grows like theirs. When you see a rag, your thoughts will run out to appropriate it. If you live with lecherous men but a moment, when you see a girl, your thoughts will run after her. Renounce the love of the world and its entangling snares. I have but one thing to tell you, says Tukā, Sing the consort of Rukmini.

3470

YOU cannot make a bow of a pestle, or extract juice from a stone by squeezing it. A barren woman will never yield milk, nor a flint grow soft if you boil it. The mirage will never fertilize the nine continents; you cannot force a mountain to touch the sky. The perishable body will never become Bramha. If you try to bring such things about, says Tukā, you will be wasting your pains.

3471

VERBAL knowledge is far removed from this secret; motions of the hand and spells will not bestow the experience which is needed. Joy and anger roll in on us like waves; lust and wrath leave us on the shore of the stream. Devotion will not succeed at Viṭṭhobā's feet, unless we have renounced the world. Tukā says, Bliss comes when we throw off the body; as we meditate on him, time after time, we become merged in him.

3472

WERE food of all the six flavours cooked and spread on potsherds and set in public places in the dead of night, men of principle would never touch it; dogs would devour it at their leisure. Even so, the worshippers of Hari look on wicked actions; they have given up their love of sensual pleasures; they look on this world, yea, and the next, as polluted places. Tukā says, This service is what I delight in; fulfil my desire for it, day by day.

3473

ALL the world is false and illusive; I have no power to discern the real. It is all legerdemain, and I think it all genuine; as I look upon it, it all vanishes. I am now grieved within me; tell me speedily of some remedy. I see not what is to become of me; I have laid my head at thy feet. Save me, O Infinite One, says Tukā.

XVII

The Saints

I.—Their Character

3474

TRUE happiness in thc world is to be penniless; Hari's people are one kin. Their steadfast courage cannot be crushed; their devotion is a sentiment that never fails. Be they hungry or thirsty, they ever remember God. Tukā says, These are they whose wealth is their own Nārāyaṇa.

3475

THE knowledge of Bramha comes with piteous cries to their doors; but the servants of Vishṇu treat it lightly. It tries to force its way in, but they drive it away. Tukā says, No efforts are needed here; it falls on the neck of those who are indifferent to it.

3476

YOU may call a woman mad with passion, when she tears off her clothes and strips herself naked. What significance belongs to mere talk?

Inside and outside mean different things. The sight or even the taste of the mirage will not satisfy thirst. You may call him stout-hearted who goes on his way without waiting for anyone. Tukā says, These are the characteristics which form the ornaments worn by the saints.

3476 a

COME, plunder this bliss of love, take your fill of it. If one misses it, he is ruined; the migrations he has passed through are wasted. The Vaishnāvas have surrendered their own souls and assaulted Vaikuntha; they have put Time to flight. They have brought heaven down to earth, with Vitho the chief thereof; his heart is pierced with arrows of his names, and he is led captive. Merits past, present, and to come are all buried deep; they are driven forth as feeble creatures into exile. The Vaishnāvas shout with overflowing joy, they raise a cry without ceasing; the demons tremble; these heroes submit to none. We have gotten freely what Bramha could not compass; wake up, says Tukā, and grasp it.

3477

WE should not kill even a snake in the presence of the saints, since they feel that their own souls pervades the universe. There is one thread that runs through the individual and the universal soul; both are indistinguishable; if you pluck forth a single hair, the whole body feels a shock. The saints cannot bear to see another hurt; it is a sort of pain to themselves ; they feel that the soul in all creatures is the same. Tukā says, This is the law of morality ; this is what is meant by worship ; it keeps the soul at peace.

3478

THY suppliants are men of glorious splendour. God suffers them not to be left away from him ; through the power of their faith, they have an assured place in him. They possess all knowledge, yet they are as though they knew nothing. God himself becomes a desire within their minds. Tukā says, A life of infant ignorance is best ; the mother feeds her baby from her breast.

3479

THEY captured God by an effort of strength, destroying the limitations of the world. They made it their first principle to scorn the elements and the race of men ; thus they made themselves lords of mankind. Tukā says, In this matter, impatience is wrong ; experience will bring you the knowledge of this sweetness.

3480

WHEN a mother-cow eats her fill in a pasture, the calf in her womb expects no call to feed. Even so, when we honour the Vaishnāvas, the god within them is contented. A father delights in the triumphs of his son. Tukā says, When nectar is placed before us, all hunger, all maladies vanish.

3481

'FEAR not',—these were their words.

3482

WE servants of Vishṇu mark our foreheads with white clay; that is what we wear. These are the jewels we display, the ornaments given us by our lord. We have been sold to serve him with our souls; by faith, single-hearted and unblemished. Tukā says, We have grown brave; we have left the world.

3483

THE *bauhinia* and the *mimosa*, with forest-grass, make up a bunch that is honoured on Dasrā day. So, too, respect is showed to a man for the sake of God; were it not so, who would pay any heed to him? A clay vessel is placed on the head for the sake of the water it holds. Tukā says, Observe that wooden measures are given and taken, when they have grain in them.

II.—Their services to men

3484

TO-DAY, O ye saints, my father and mother, you have given me a gift of your favour. Words sweet as nectar have risen to my lips; I can never, in this life, repay you. You are generous and merciful, says Tukā; in fond love for your child, you have covered him with ornaments.

3485

O YE saints, make everything of mine acceptable; the burden rests on you. Once I strayed about, but I brought this to a close at your feet; I stir from them no more. Tukā says, I have loosened the knot; I have embraced your feet.

3486

CHILDREN control their mother through the love she bears them; does she minister to their wants through any design of her own? Do you then, O ye saints, ignore my shortcomings as she does theirs. The mother puts up with her children's prattle and tricks, and anon she embraces them; is this, says Tukā, because she has no power to control them? Yet no harsh impulse arises in her.

3487

TUKĀ says, My body is comforted when particles of their dust fall on it.

3488

WHATEVER a man eats himself, the same he gives away to beggars. Go, then, to ask a morsel where the saints live. Then your belly will be filled, and there will be food too left behind. Tukā says, Thus all searching, all desire will come to an end.

3489

'TIS well to make your own dwelling-place where the saints live. They wake up the sleepy; they give you abundantly the true self. To live with them and live like them should be your only vocation. Profit brings forth further profit; one spirit testifies to another. Nothing unpropitious interferes with this. 'Tis well, says Tukā, to take measures which will bring the saints to our houses.

3490

I HAVE not revealed this spell to anyone; I have clasped it to my soul; I have set my mind on the brick in a spirit of faith. Tukā says, They who searched out salvation in earlier days have left behind them this stay for others.

3491

HOW can I say what I owe to the saints? Good counsel is their natural and wonted speech; they labour to teach men. Tukā says, As the cow is always thinking of the calf, so do they protect me.

3492

TUKĀ says, How can I pay back what I owe the saints?

3493

TO help the children, the teacher holds a slate in his hand. Even so, in this world, the saints act themselves to set forth an example.

The mother knows the gait of her little children, and makes her own steps conform to it. Tukā says, A boat is placed in water to be useful to men.

3494

HIS attributes are infinite; though we attempt to describe them, we cannot fathom them; he, the home of the saints, is beyond our reach. No, you cannot find the home where the saints themselves dwell. Find where the saints are, and fix your eyes on them, making no idle clamour about the matter. Become a saint yourself, and then look for the saints; then alone you can be saved, says Tukā.

III.—The insignificance of caste in comparison of virtue

3495

YOU are holy men; you have been set apart; we *shudras* will not stand in your path. What is the use of false pride on either side? Contemplation of God is all-sufficient; what good will it do us to associate with exalted men? Tukā says, Give me not, O God, any service displeasing to thee.

3496

GLORY, princely power, and wealth let us renounce, and beg our bread from door to door. Let us first secure our true welfare; this is what the rules of conduct enjoin on us. Pride in caste or lineage, worldly honour we should renounce. Tukā says, Betake yourself to solitude, lay aside all hesitation, shout out your defiance of death.

3497

IF an onion springs up on a pediment for the *tulsi* it pleases thee not, O Govinḍa, whatever we do for it. So too, men void of devotion, though born in high ranks, we should look on as demons, as the scentless core of the *ketaka* flower. Tukā says, A maggot in a piece of sandal-wood will never be placed on God's forehead.

XVIII

Appeals and Exhortations

3498

GO forth, shouting out the roll of his names; as the worshipper progresses in this joy, he meets Gopala. Roll on the ground, and reverence the dust on the saints' feet. Raise your arms, says Tukā, that Viṭṭhala may come speedily.

3498 a

THE body will pass away; thou stone, understandest thou not? What are elephants, horses, palaces, quilts, couches, and pillows? When old age comes along, they will bring shame on you. Thy kith and kin are but as cranes that eat up the harvest. Awake ere it is too late, says Tukā; there is danger ahead of you!

3499

MAKE him thy god alone; all others are part of illusion, sources of misery; from first to last, there is nothing abiding in them. Make the eternal to be part of thyself, by passionate love of Govinḍa. Then, says Tukā, one death will end all, and you will leave a glorious name behind you.

3500

WHETHER you speak words of praise or blame, speak them of God; wicked is he who idly wastes speech on other topics. Those who listen to such speech grow deaf; they pay money to enter hell. Yes, in this world, men will spit on them; and they will have to live in hell hereafter. Tukā says, Speech is an honest measure; but the censure of others fills it with hell.

3501

WE have started out on an auspicious day; who will go back now? Be things as they may, if we have to sacrifice our body, what need we care? The soul is in constant dread over the possessions that fall to its lot. How is it, O God, says Tukā, that we pass our life in misery?

3502

UNDOUBTEDLY, it is best we should meet a great man face to face. We should not die like cowards; the life of the coward is wretched.

We should plunder this inexhaustible treasure. Tukā says, We should so live as to shed lustre pre-eminent upon our name.

3503

IF we can attain to devotion, it matters not what happens to our lives. You should not let any kind of fear stand in your path. Leave nothing untried to prove yourself the equal of any man. Be a hero, says Tukā, a leader by the leader's side.

3504

EVEN nectar, if a man dislikes it, will not stay on the stomach; whereas poison becomes a necessary to the man accustomed to it. When we offer a cocoanut, the thing of value is not the nut, but the honour for which it stands; the cocoanut is acceptable when it is accompanied by a kindly spirit and good intentions. Good habits are natural to one who is sincere; but if you enforce them, will they take root? Tukā says, Follow natural inclination in all your proceedings; we have leisure and patience on our side.

3505

THE fitness or purity of our mind, the mind itself can testify; there is no need for any one to inform it on this point. If you mean to be truly brave, you must be ready to sacrifice your life. You will then enjoy bliss beyond measure; both lord and people alike will honour you. Tukā says, As is the speech, such is the impression it makes.

3506

I HAVE suffered in many rebirths; I have died of hunger; but this was my best friend in the world. Look after yourself; look after yourself, for the body is perishable, and you have not yet bestirred yourself to set it free from illusion. Even she who fed thee with a morsel from her mouth becomes a stranger to thee; it is not that she does not grieve for thee, but she cannot release thee. Tukā says, By wealth, and honour, and the sense of self have I been corrupted; the world did not suffer me to see the gain that now I possess.

3507

THE praises of men end in the utter ruin of our lives; if we lose sight of Nārāyaṇa, whatever we do is sinful. He gave us our lives; we are guilty, says Tukā, if we listen to any speech that derogates from his honour.

3508

TAKE the road to Pāndhari before Time assaults and falls upon you. Your senses will grow feeble in the hour of sunset; so, while your hands and feet and jaws are free to move, bethink yourself. Why are you taken up with vain desires? Of what are you dreaming? Tukā says, When will you come by such a treasure again?

3509

BUY something brother! Be it much or little. Here, in this very market, examine your purchase and tie it up in your bundle. Spend your money while there are still goods before you; afterwards, you will have to put up with imitations. The shop is open now; when night has fallen, who will let you in? Tukā says, In the last hour, your jaws will be fast closed.

3510

IT has grown cheap, it has come from the port to our house. Be now greedily desirous of it; very sweet is this juice of devotion. Take but a step towards it, and all anxious care will leave you; Tukā says, No trouble about merits or demerits can linger on.

3511

IF a man shows a road to another, what does he lose by this? But if another goes by the wrong road in spite of warning, he is ruined. How many people have gone wrong in this way! In spite of warnings, they ate poison. If a man looks carefully round him, he will not lose his life, he will not perish. Tukā says, If a man is weary of life, what can be done for him, O Keshāva?

3512

WHEREFORE art thou tormented by endless desires? Why dost thou not submit thyself to God? As thou art, thou dost keep thy thoughts fixed on men as earnestly as a heron watches fish. Why dost thou not trust God as earnestly as thou dost now entangle thyself in love for thy children? Why dost thou not find God as sweet to thee as the wife that strips thee of thy goods? Why dost thou not show God the same gratitude thou showest to the spirits of thy fathers, when thou worshipest them with false and burdensome rites? Why dost thou live in dread of the world, forgetting Nārāyaṇa? Why has thou wasted all thy life, says Tukā, spending it without devotion?

3513

A GAJARA woman sets off to bring water home; her thoughts are fixed on her pot of water, she walks with her dress loose, her attention is given to the pot. A boy sends a kite up into the sky, he keeps hold of the string; the kite seems to be far away, but his attention is fixed on it. A thief carries off a treasure and buries it in a forest; he lives amongst men and things, but his thoughts are with the treasure. An adulteress looks after her house; but her love follows her paramour, her thoughts are with him. Tukā says, Wherever we are busy, we should not let our thoughts stray from the Lord of All.

3514

YOUR comrades depart one after another; how can you imagine yourself secure? What will you do when you are left alone, and the hour has drawn nigh? Be then at least so far vigilant as to set yourself free. Ears, hair, and eyes,—these are slowly taking leave of you. Your teeth are dwindling in number, your jaws tremble; all that is left is your tongue lolling about helplessly. All these, says Tukā, have compassed your downfall.

3515

WE have traced him and pursued him; now we have gained an eternal share in him. He has come to your house from far away; now, strive to make him your own. These treasures have been broken open; all suddenly, we have caught sight of them. Seize now, says Tukā, sufficient for one and all of you.

3516

WHAT is the mouth but a storehouse for corn or a den for beasts, if it does not constantly utter thy name? Tukā says, The best life is that which is not lived one moment without Pānduranga.

3517

LIVE not with those that esteem themselves saints, lest any of their qualities cling to you. You could not then avoid the guilt you would incur; it would swallow up all your good deeds. Tukā says, Salute such people from afar; keep firmly placed in your heart his form.

3518

HAVE we spent all our days in festivities, that we are not free to begin the *kathā*? The true root of our guilt is that we take no delight in it; how then can it be called the path of salvation? It is mere dust. What is left men out of all the treasures they store up? Can they take it when they leave the world for a single moment?

Nay, rather, burnish up your speech, churn forth jewels of words. Tukā says, Let your delight be in uttering this; it may be difficult for both of us, but it ensures our true welfare.

3519

YAMA shows no honour to any one; why then are you ashamed to utter the name of Rāma? He will set you free when you are caught in the grip of time; who is there that has ever escaped it? They have gone to boil and shriek in the pot of hell. If you desire your own welfare, then utter the name of Viṭṭhala. He who will not do so, says Tukā, will know the consequences when he suffers them.

3520

WHEN people sit devoutly listening to a *kathā* and converse happily concerning God, what wonder is it that the speaker rescues and saves others by the sweet perfume of his words? Should he spoil the *kathā* by his slothfulness, or destroy the spirit of it by caviling, he would sink himself and defile the ship of salvation. Good people are like sandal-wood; but we should keep away from the bad, even if we have to leave their country. Let Hari dwell with you; such is the request Tukā makes.

3521

WHY do you not worship Hari—who but he will accept you? In Yama's city there will be the chastisements of Yama, the torments of hell.

What impatience is troubling you? What will you do when you get there? Why do you swell with pride? Will they handle you respectfully when they drag you along the road? Your mouth will be gagged, your tongue will be pulled out; why do you fear the reproaches of men,—who will save you? Be ashamed, says Tukā; do not waste your life.

3522

WE ought to bestow a gift on such as crave for one; there is true merit in the act. What is to happen, is welcome to occur; only let it bring wisdom with it. That your views may be true, kindle a light like sunlight in your heart. Tukā says, Let there be space enough within my mind to preserve pure faith there.

3523

TO do a good business is our welfare; we must exert all our powers at the right moment. It is not certain if we shall make a gain or a loss; both accrue unexpectedly; give the matter your careful thought, then take what steps are necessary. Add fuel to the fire at the right moment; don't over-cook the food; if each man dines separately, then each one gets which suits him best. Turn up the field with the plough, harrow it, weed it, make it smooth. Tukā says, Bring in the sheaves at last, and store them.

3524

THE mind knows its own welfare; it recognizes the correct thing to do. Concealment of aims is hypocrisy; it is truthfulness that effects them. Base metal cannot pass the test; it melts in the fire. Tukā says, Make and keep a genuine article; it will serve you well in time to come.

3525

WHEN a man has long followed the wrong path, he turns back at last; he is quit of the fear that he felt up till then. We should not lose sight of the chief point; the end, when we reach it, will be full of sweetness. When we have done with desires, what is there left to excite us? In early days, it was the way of men to gird up their loins in due season; in those days, guilt lost its power, because men repented of it. Tukā says, Our reason helps us when we secure its help; God stands close beside us, waiting for us to call on him.

3526

AUSPICIOUS is a store of auspicious objects; we can never grow sick of it, it can never bring loss on us. Store them up while they are in the market place; 'Excellent', 'excellent', you should say of them. Janārdana dwells in the world; in this market-place we see him unadulterated. Tukā says, When many mouths attest the genuine article, you should store it up at your convenience.

3527

IF the prince does not punish evil-doers, rogues will give much trouble to other men. If the cultivators do not look after their fields and weed them, how will they gather in any grain? Tukā says, Holy men should do nothing wrong; they will avoid sin by considering what is right.

3528

WHAT do you lose if you simply close your mouth? What do you gain if you insist on 'I' 'I'? Do but sit like a dolt in your own house; let no one speak to any one else. Tukā says, I tell you what to do; sit still, and fix your thoughts on God.

3529

AS children tie a string to a bee's foot, so you will find yourself tied up; then who will set you free? Men tie a monkey by a string, and march him round from door to door. Tukā says, See how yon captive bear goes coughing along.

3530

WHEN you wake every morning, you think of nothing but food; you forget your true welfare. Yet, when you were conceived in your mother's womb, even then He took due care of you. The clouds never fail to pour down rain for the *chataka* bird; how then will he leave you disappointed? The birds and wild creatures that live on the earth, Hari never forgets them. Tukā says, Keep faith firm within your mind, then the consort of Lakshmī will not forget you.

3531

I KNOW one, a wealthy man, who is suffering from leprosy, black or white; another who is blind or dumb. The ways of Fate are fantastic and unsearchable; the strings of the puppets are in Viṭṭhobā's hand. There are other diseases, past numbering, that constantly invade such men. Tukā says, They bring this gift that they destroy men's *Karma*, but they have no pleasure in the gift.

3532

WHILE you are busy at work, utter the name of Rāma; the wrong of life will pass away, your sorrow will be turned to ease. You will find out this in your last hour, when your breath is failing you, when you are parted from wife and children and everything. You may get through life somehow or other, but there is a whirlpool ahead of you; break the snares off you, and do what you have to do. Whatever you have done in this life, you will still depend entirely on Viṭṭhobā's name; if you burn up your *Karma*, you will be saved, says Tukā.

3533

DO as I bid you do; why do you go down to hell? That alone is a holy action wherein Nārāyana is found. God protects those who seek his protection; others are assaulted by fierce disorders. Tukā says, Cling to him; faith will show you what his secret is.

3534

TUKA says, By many means and ways, embrace him with your soul, all of you.

3535

A SESAMUM-SEED, half a grain of mustard, a grain of boiled rice, should you gain as much happiness as that, you will find, if you look, that it has no bounds. So, make haste; do not waste your time looking round you, while we possess all our senses and all are fully awake. To-day we have our fill of happiness, a happiness with which holy-places cannot compare, not even those that are above Kashi or Gaya. Whoso, through pride, is ashamed to accept this, in this matter, says Tukā, he will be ruined.

3536

THE stones were magic stones, the ground was of gold, he was connected by lineage with the Upholder of the World. His town was of gold surrounded by the sea; he had a great host of demons. Ten times eight thousand were his wives; the chief of his queens was Mandodari. His sons and grandsons who can count? The chief of his sons prevailed over Indra. Fourteen ages he lived; his brother was Kumbhakarna. Though all the gods were his slaves, says Tukā, he took away with him not a cowri when he perished.

3537

IF a man has been driven away from the saints, should he wish to keep company with you, depart from him and live quietly by yourself. Burn up that place where there is no thought of the Supreme. There is no peace of mind there, says Tukā.

3538

AFTER many lives, you have at last been born a man; now make yourself a friend of God. Good sir, make now your true welfare your own object; seek your profit no more in unprofitable deeds. Give up now the path of crooked designs; there is a strait road before you to Pāndhari. The very source of joy stands there upright on a brick. Tukā shouts his name aloud.

3539

IN the market of liberation, a full store of goods is set forth; carry on a roaring trade. Come, all kinsmen of ours, buy on credit, buy on credit! There is no division of ranks here; none are great or small. Tukā says, Make a profit here; look after your capital of faith.

3540

A MOMENT spent with Nārāyana he looks on as suffering; death, which is due to-morrow, he brings on to-day, and says, 'It is all a matter of luck'. God will not allow you to want anything; be assured, he will stand by you in the last hour. Consider within yourself where your true welfare lies, and be awake when the end approaches. Your cravings and wild desires, such as are left, bundle up and tie to your waist. Enough of your present ways! They will not suffice you in the last hour; your life of youth and strength will not last for ever. Give up then your disgust for religion,—the crude offspring of ignorance,—or hope, and thirst, and illusion will grow strong upon you. When this body nears its end, its clay will grow heavy and last but a moment. What you call your own will be foreign to you; the sight of your nose and eyes will make you sick. Till these miseries come upon you, your life and your future are in your power. Tukā says, If you think well what your true gain is, all entanglements will be found treacherous.

3541

HOW shameless is he who dies unsaved, though he was born with wisdom. He does not renounce the world at a blow; he endures all its hardships, and rubs himself when bruised by them. Tukā wakes you up, O sleepy ones! Listen to me!

3542

DO not be infatuated by wife, son, or wealth. The hours, as they pass, are swallowed up by time. O man! What means of salvation have you secured? Offer all your body, says Tukā, to the Lord of the World.

3543

THIS is a haunt of robbers; they wander round your homes day and night—how many sleepy people they have plundered before now! Market-dealers, all of you, look after your goods! Keep on the look-out, watch the people who are asleep by your side. Keep wide-awake, and take your own profits home with you. Ho! travellers, guards and criers, perform your task, take care of your brethren! We shall wake you up with Hari's name; look out, says Tukā.

3544

NO creature born into the world stays there long; death sits close beside his pillow. Look at the mouse,—the cat carries him off; so, too, does death carry off mankind. Look at the kid in the butcher's house; how can a cow continue alive with one who sells beef? Tukā says, Draw some profit from time; the passing hour will not come back.

3545

YOU are like a two-days' guest that walks with his head in the air; why do you not worship Nārāyana? You are for ever gloomy till the hand of death suddenly carries you off; when will you worship the lord of Pāndhari? Countless such people there are, says Tukā; when will they meet Keshava, who reigns above all?

XIX

Rebukes and Admonitions

I.—The evil age

3546

BEHOLD now the triumph of the age of Kali; the world delights in iniquity; it spurns the saints and consents to sin. So strong has impiety grown, that all mankind are deluded; piety has been rooted out, and the dissolution of all things has set in. Truly, this age is astounding; forgetting the high principles of a Bramhāna's duty, the first-born resort to Dāvalapira. Truth has been forsaken for falsehood; the highest truth has been swamped; righteousness never came to this pass before; some evil demon has spread his power abroad. Peace, mercy, compassion, devotion, good deeds,—we need not even mention them; truth and courage have vanished. The duties proper to age and station are forgotten; men pursue what is not their own business; they consider it a burden to call out Rāma Rāma! They run after a comic actor, like a goblin after an oblation; but mention to them a *katha* or a *purâna*, and the lazy wretches at once find themselves in pain. In their greed for pleasure and gain, they would sacrifice everything,—even life itself; but ask them for a handful of flour in return for the Highest, and they will fly at you like dogs. Let them catch sight of a rich man—be he a nameless outcast,—and infallibly they will treat him with respect; but no respect do they show to such as recite the Vedas,—good men learned in all the Scriptures. Sons suffer their fathers to serve them as though they were servants; mothers-in-law have become the bond-slaves of their daughters. Falsehood spreads; Vimvasi triumphs; all sense of propriety is gone; wives treat their husbands as though they were beggars. Men are too proud to salute the servants of Hari; for their belly's sake, they will bow down to a buffoon of the Mlenchhas. Sin has grown wild and wanton; men are so wilful that they hold nothing good; they eat unlawful food; none esteems any man's touch a pollution. They take food on the eleventh day, yea Brāmhanas do so, and chew betel after it, and speak the language of Musalmanas. Ladies of birth have been dishonoured, while men kiss the faces of slaves; yet they make a boast of their purity, and parade their sanctity before the eyes of the world. Men love spirits, no one cares for butter; whores go strutting about, while chaste women live in misery. Men have put merit out of sight, and brought shame on saints and holy-places. In horror at all this, the showers from the clouds have shrunk ; the earth is wasted and trembles. The gods have shut themselves up ; there is a struggle for life everywhere. Day by day, crops are falling off ; cattle yield less milk ; towns look deserted. There is a plentiful crop of heresies ; offerings and oblations have been forgotten ; sacrifices and vows, the repetition of holy names and penance ; corruption has spread abroad. Brāmhaṇas follow the eighteen trades ; they have even begun to steal ; they have left off their white clothes, and wear blue. They have given up the Gita and the Gayatri ; there is a crowd of wonder-workers dealing in spells ; Vedic reciters sell their daughters as though they were horses. As for the Vedas, they turn them into ridicule ; learned men delight in Mahommedan priests. Unimpeachable courses of life have been crushed and impoverished ; vile wretches are flaunting their tricks, and frauds, and deceits. Men show their adroitness and skill in disputes, bickerings, and aspersions ; by debates over the prescribed and the prohibited men are made dupes. Religious ascetics, that should have renounced all passions, clothes, and desires, are brimful of lust and anger and never struggle to be free from the grip of desire. Astounding is this age of Destruction ; kings destroy their subjects ; fathers, sons and brothers treat each other like foes. How mighty is this whore of time ! She has thrown all mankind into a whirl of error ; she has mixed and corrupted the eighteen vocations and the four castes. We have seen with our eyes what the saints foretold. Now let all this pass ; in this age of Kali, it is idle to follow any rules of conduct ; we must call on God for mercy, and remember him in our hearts. O Lord of Vaikunṭha! Why dost thou look on all this as a mere diversion? While Kali tortures mankind, O run to help them; Tukā's servant cries aloud to thee.

3547

IN a village full of impious men, what can a saint do? He is like a cow shut up in a tiger's den. In a street full of butchers, if you swear by a bull and offer that as an assurance, what is it worth? Plantain trees and thorn bushes may grow near each other, but what intercourse can there be between them? Tukā says, If you make pottage of bitter seeds, how can it be sweet or wholesome.

3548

IN this Kali age, a Brāmhana carries on business as a usurer; he rambles about the quarters of Mahars and Mangs. In driving a bargain with a Mang from the hills, he pays no heed to the pollution of his touch. He settles his accounts every day with a Mang woman; her spittle falls upon his face. He writes down on paper the names of whores like Ashā Māyā; he never remembers Nārāyana. Tukā says, His body is in a stranger's power; but a prosperous consummation only Pānduranga can give.

3549

THOUGH born to a Brāmhana's part, he carries on a business in usury; he wanders from one *Chandala's* door to another. He begs rice from men of the lowest castes, and the gift he bestows upon them is abuse of their mothers and sisters. He is born in the highest station, but his actions are vile; he sinks his whole family into hell. Such is the practice of the Kali age, says Tukā; in their selfishness, men drown the principles of conduct.

3550

TELL me, what service shall I render thee? We are ruined by pedantry, O God! Thy secret we cannot penetrate now; unless thou shouldst tell it me, I look to be ruined. Rules for ablution and conduct are abolished. 'What is there in them?' people say. Adoration is abolished. 'Images are stones,' they say; 'men have set them up to get food for their own bodies.' 'Men should neither preach nor fast,' they say; public worship has been abolished. 'Men should not visit temples; they have God in their own homes'. Thus, says Tukā, they have ruined everything.

3551

I TELL you the fruit of the Kali age; a general confusion lies before the world. Men will call us thorns,—such is the practice they will set up. They will worship women, and give them liquor to drink; any man will visit any woman he pleases. The highest castes, to whom Vedic learning belongs, will take flesh and strong drink. The four castes and the eighteen sub-castes will sit and eat in one row together. They will call this a wave of Bhavānī's diversion; they will say that all men are Śiva embodied. This will come to pass, I prognosticate the same; I tell you it before I pass away. Tukā serves his teacher; mystic powers do all bear water to his house.

3552

'O HUSBAND! what shall I do? You have left me with a baby. My husband has died suddenly; whom has he left to take care of me? Don't break my door down; I will cut his hands and feet off.' She seized him by the beard with one hand, and an axe she takes in the other. She is just about to strike when he rises to his feet! Tukā says, All mankind are thieves; in the last hour, your only true friend is the name of Rāma.

II.—The obstinacy and folly of the wicked

3553

WHEN a man is remiss in his duties, then Kali descends upon him. It will go ill with him in the end; live, then, in fear of this. Kali will twist thy ear and throttle thee,—beware! Let none think that Tukā will remain silent.

3554

THIS lad spent twelve years in childish games, such as tipcat, cricket, quoits, 'riders', *champī*, *peṇda*, *khaḍi*, '*ēki-bēki*, *hamāma*, *humbari*, *pakavyāchā*, *bāra*, peg-tops, and kissing peg-tops, *seladērā*, spinning round, stone-lifting; thus his childhood passed, says Tukā, then came youth, the root of pride.

3555

IN the arrogance of youth, he respected nobody, but puffed himself up like a bull. With careful pains, punctiliously, he tied his turban; he stalked about among people like a buffalo. A triple-folded cloth on his arm, his head erect, he showed no respect to virtuous people. Like a dog, he roamed from door to door, casting sinful glances at women. Tukā says, Such a disorderly rogue was he; he passed his life in idle pranks.

3556

IN old age come colds, catarrhs, and coughs; a man sits, resting his forehead on his hand. His face looks like half a dry cocoanut; his nose runs copiously. He cannot utter a single word correctly; his breath gurgles through congested phlegm. His neighbour says, 'Why doesn't the wretch die? We are sick of him.' Lay aside everything else, says Tukā, and remember Rāma every moment.

18

3557

THE company of men increases our troubles; it makes worship impossible; mankind, O God, are of three sorts. Thus, I am weary of society; I observe their varied interests; there is no room there for single-hearted faith; uncertainty prevents the growth of it. The learned do not see their own true welfare; when they meet other men they dislike them. Tukā says, Solitude is best for us.

3558

THE touch of the magic stone has changed a sickle into gold; it keeps its curved form, but its value is not diminished thereby. When the *senda* ripens, it loses the qualities it had; will any one despise it now? Tukā says, Even *surana* can be served up at the table, for cooking changes its properties.

3559

THE kith and kin of a whore, that would pity a thief, they grow like him through contact with him. They set up thorns on their own path, and enter the way of sorrow without any compensation. To feed a snake is to spoil good milk, it merely turns nectar into poison. Tukā says, Unless you punish people like these, you will not be able to check the faults of those that come after them.

3560

IF a man's mind is filled with thoughts about his own body, he will delight in honour paid him by the world. Such a one is in great danger in the market-place; thieves untie his bundle and carry off his goods. Yet even when he has lost them, he is not free; his neck is fast bound by pretensions and greed. Henceforth, his business is ruined; ruin has plainly overtaken him. Tukā says, So the saints declare; why then does any one wittingly ruin himself?

3561

YOU may dig a trench round a neem-tree, and fill it with sugar; it will not cease to produce its own natural fruit. Even so, the mind of the wicked is defiled; he vomits up what is best for him. Touch a potsherd with the magic-stone; it will not change its own nature. Tukā says, Do not bamboos grow close to sandal-trees?

3562

IN hot desire for the world, his feet carry him on thievish errands afar; now, what will be the end of him? He is like one whose food is not duly cooked. Though he eats it, he vomits it up time after time; what bodily vigour can he retain? Tukā says, If a man has not faith, his toil ends in the affliction of men.

3563

IT is not known to fools that greedy desire is followed by piteous complaints. 'Don't burn my pots'; there is fear in his heart, and expressions of greed on his lips. When death overtakes us, what will any strength avail us? A man piles up merit and demerit; it ends in this, that he goes to hell when he is dead. 'How can I avoid doing good to others'? this is what he is always thinking. Tukā says, This is truly wolfish greed; may we never meet with it!

3564

SOME men are insolent by nature, steeped and dyed in insolence; keep far away from them! Back or front, how can poison end in anything wholesome? Tukā says, My friend, a snake doesn't understand that you are stroking him lovingly.

3565

A MAN bound by hopes is void of shame; he says, the fruit will slowly ripen; he waits for it. To gain his purposes, he overlooks his own degradation; his mind finds its source of contentment in gain. Tukā says, Though you gave him a push, he would not admit it; he closes his eyes.

3566

THEY offer vows to the stone gods that they will swing themselves from hooks, but they will not let their wives attend a *katha*. They spend heaps of wealth on tombs, but they treat as ill-omened the pediment for the *tulsi* that stands at their doors. When they are plundered by thieves, they feel no great pang ; but they will not drop a coin in a Bramhāna's hand. They entertain their relatives by marriage, but turns their backs on those that seek a charitable dole. Tukā says, They are like beasts of burden, that do not know the reason why they toil.

3567

HE is puffed up with pride ; he will no more bend than a rod of iron. Cannot the dull clod recognize his true advantage, even though you dash it in his face ? When his soul departs, he will grow stiff in death ; his eyes will be staring wide-open ; Tukā says, If you try to use a pestle as a bow, you will make nothing of it.

3568

HE runs after the drudgery of worldly life ; how he loves it ! When he goes out to ease himself, he picks up stones ; he thinks over his worldly projects. All that he is ashamed of is Nārāyana's name ; he is willing to talk nonsense to children. Tukā says, O shameless wretch, you make a boast of your toils and cares.

3569

WE should shun the company of the wicked, for it breaks the spirit, time after time. Though a snake be not moving, we should not call it a harmless creature; it will attack us at once, if provoked. Tukā says, Keep the wicked far from you; take steps to avoid speaking to them.

3570

I KNOW not how long these wretches must bear the drudgery of life; care and anxiety dwell for ever in their hearts. While their lips are idle, what pains would it cost them to cry Rāma? They turn aside from this and delude themselves; they are entangled by the intoxicating pleasures of sense. Though they know this, they know it not; their open eyes they have closed; the storm of illusion fills them, and works its will in them. Such men, says Tukā, assuredly are void of sense; there may be differences between them, but they all merge into the same character.

3571

MEN find room in themselves for the great object, but they cannot bear the long toil needed to reach it. The laden animal grunts at its degrading task, as it turns the mill where its wretched earnings are made. Though he has a white flower near his nose, he spits, under the pretext that he perceives an evil smell. Tukā says, How many people cannot profit by counsel!

3572

A MAN whose nose has been cut off is startled to see himself in a glass; he turns aside his face in shame. Even so is a man appalled by his own inner qualities. A thief prefers dark nights, and is annoyed when he sees the moon rise. Tukā says, Mankind are luckless creatures, O God!

3573

THEY look on strings of gems as though they were glass; they despise them, and put them aside on their own judgment. The bent of their minds interferes with their eye-sight; their ignorance brings a loss on them. They look on the cow of wishes as though it were a common cow or buffalo; and a common cow they look on as if she were the other. Tukā says, Why need I say much about them? Their practices are suited to themselves.

3574

A KNAVISH Bramhāna who torments other men, if you bestow a gift on such a man, you will, both of you, go to hell. Yes, that is what happens to both in such a case,—to the one who asks and the other who encourages him; branches rubbing against each other set the woods on fire. If you carve a boat out of stone, you waste your money and labour; there is no place where a ship of that kind would float; it would drown its passengers. Even if you give funds to a thief, he will plunder on the high roads. Tukā says, It would be a piece of ostentation on the part of the giver, and would ruin both of them.

3575

HOW much advice is needed to influence a rogue? He does not like anything that will do him good. Why are there no pure desires in the wretch? He has burned up the merit of his good actions. He has no faith within him; he will not listen to words; he only weakens himself. Tukâ says, Why did his mother bring him forth? He is always talking nonsense, so it seems.

3576

YOU may decorate an ass, and devote fond attention to him; he will never be a horse, whatever you do. He will never stop braying; how can he help his own nature? You may seat a dog in a litter; but he will not stop his aimless barking. Tukā says, These actions are natural to the creatures; whatever you do, a habit cannot be shaken off.

3577

A MAN takes no pleasure in a mirror, if his nose is not found on his face. So too, says Tukā, a rogue turns away from spiritual instruction.

3578

THE ideas of the wicked are such that he is for ever reviling the saints. If a man remembers Rāma, he calls him a useless fool; if a man goes on pilgrimage, he calls him a beggar. Tukā says, A scorpion has but one sting; a wicked man has stings all over his body.

3579

THOUGH you cast a net into the sea, it cannot hold a drop of water. Even such is a sinner's mind; he loves not the service of God. You may bathe an ass in Ganges water, but he goes and rolls on a dunghill. You may feed a crow affectionately, but he will go and roll on filth. So too, says Tukā, a hog is never fond of musk.

3580

NO one can boil and cook food in a broken pot. The touch of the magic stone cannot change a potsherd, no matter how hard you rub it. Like water poured on an inverted pot is a *katha* in the ears of the wicked, says Tukā.

3581

ADVICE is wasted on the wicked; their sinful minds will not obey rules of behaviour; their pretences are like ornaments on widows. Their morose temper will listen to nothing; 'Why should I worry myself in vain'? What use is there in smearing an ass with sandal, or putting saffron on the forehead of a pig? You may give any amount of advice to an adultress, but she looks on it all as false doctrine. Tukā says, Preaching to a man without faith is but a waste of labour.

3582

AT a preaching, he sleeps all the time; when talk about women is going on, he keeps himself awake. Tukā says, Do not be angry with him; who can help his own nature?

3583

A SINNER never thinks of his own past; he blames God for every evil. He commits mountains of sins, and feels no fear; he is a wicked, abject wretch. He never remembers his own vile conduct, but he blames God for his troubles. May thorns pierce his face, says Tukā.

3584

THEY know the truth, but they cannot escape from their entanglements; their food does not digest within them. Their souls are a dower of egoism bestowed on them; the compassion I have bestowed on them is wasted. These proud creatures have but one propensity; this disposition they openly proclaim. Tukā says, How often must I declare it? Nothing stays in their mind.

3585

SWEET food is wasted on sick men, sandal on apes, camphor on crows; a noseless man loves not a mirror, nor a fool instruction in the Scriptures. Tukā says, Generous Viṭṭhala alone can lighten the darkness of the ignorant.

3586

THE sea is his father, the moon his brother, Rāma is his sister, Hari of Dvarka his brother-in-law, yet the fool goes begging from door to door. He makes his own true welfare his enemy, says Tukā.

3587

THOUGH a female ass should yield milk, could she attain to the dignity of a cow? Though a dog should be handsome, could he eat out of the same dish with you? Though an adultress should be beautiful, could we compare her to a chaste wife? Tukā says, Creatures of this kind, can they be elevated?

III.—Ill-Temper and Want of Charity

3588

HE has given up righteousness, and walks unrighteously; he talks quarrelsome nonsense everywhere. Who loses anything by this but himself? It is himself he has ruined. He censures men he ought to honour; he gives up their friendship, and nourishes a grudge against them. He prefers society of another kind; he does not move among the good. He brags of exploits, and when he brags, he asks for alms. He exalts himself, but Yama will deal harshly with him. The man who has no principles, says Tukā, is an abject wretch.

IV.—Pride

3589

PORRIDGE is made of wheat and cakes of *natchnee ;* but, in each case, good cooks are good, bad are bad. What is the use of mere reputation ? Fie on it ! It brings vexation. What effects our purposes stands out conspicuous and gains true distinction. Food is tasty when it is clean, though the mere need of food is the same in every case. Don't spoil your food ; eat as much as you want. Tukā says, What use is self-conceit to any body ? Only a straight-forward course will bring you to the true path.

V.—Deceit

3590

THE street-juggler begins a show, but does not finish it. Curse this style of life, contemptible and shameless ! When you have undertaken a rôle, you should act it to the end. Tukā says, Assuredly, God will not ignore steadfast importunity.

3591

WE can believe in a liar's invitation to dinner, when we have had a meal out of him ; to trust him otherwise would be a mistake. A female rope-dancer touches the sky in sport ; but does she thereby reach the everlasting regions ? We see riders and horses prancing on the clouds ; but would they endure on a field of battle ? Tukā says, Such is the life of the contentious ; when they speak, they bring shame on themselves.

3592 a

HE who swears falsely in court, he is a sinner in the worst degree. He will dwell, at the head of his own family, in the boiling cauldron of hell. Tukā says, He was born to bring death on his family.

VI.—Greediness

3592

A PLOT of land presented by one's forefathers, if any man ask such a thing back through greed,—though he be entitled to the place of honour amongst men,—he will suffer surpassing penalties in Yama's dwelling place. With his family on both sides, he will enter the horrors of hell. For millions of ages, says Tukā, he will encounter bars of glowing iron.

3593

WE should take no gift from a man whose wealth was acquired by greed ; we can put to no purpose such a man ; for he goes to hell. A man who sells ablutions and the holy name of God, or practices penance for spectators, that man, says Tukā, is an impostor ; he goes to hell of his own motion.

3594

I SOUGHT a teacher to advance my fortunes ; but he brought me no good. I listened to his holy words ; but my grain-pit was filled with water. I took a teacher home to live with me ; but my cattle strayed away. Give up your chattering, preacher, and let me have my sickle back. Tukā says, Wretches like these shall be doubly afflicted.

VII.—Sensuality and Love of the World

3595

THOU fool ! Thou art ashamed to greet the saints, yet thou carriest flowers to the house of a whore ! A whore, a slave, a *murali*, a pollution to the earth ! How is it thou canst think her pure ? Be ashamed, thou wanton, says Tukā ; come, beat him with the heels of your shoes.

3596

HE who thinks himself polluted by the water in which the saints' feet were washed, he whom the saints have cast out from their number,—long will he burn in hell. He who respects not the water hallowed by his teacher's feet, but drinks his fill of strong drink; who would not touch with his lips his teacher's hand, but lays his face against the face of a whore,—let his mouth, says Tukā, be filled with dirt!

3597

A POOR fool is he whose heart is such that he spends his own money to put a chain on his feet. The love of worldly pleasures destroys our life, and ruins our true interests. Deluded men make an enemy of their own body by following the suggestions of its lusts. Tukā says, The lecher ends his days in pain because he gives himself up to pleasures.

3598

'LISTEN, my daughter-in-law, don't waste the milk and curds.' The mother-in-law started for Pandharpur, but from the gate she turned back to the house. 'Listen carefully, child, to what I tell you. Take good care of any broken pots. The stack of cow-dung cakes I have piled up,—don't begin on it while I am away. The wheaten-rolls I have made and put away,—don't begin on them while I am gone. My mortar and pestle and grinding-mill,—I cannot help thinking about them.

If any beggars come to the house, tell them I am gone to Pandharpur. Eat sparingly; if you make any savings, don't waste them'. 'All right', says her daughter, 'You may go on your pilgrimage with your mind at ease. Seek your true welfare, mother; forget what you have left behind you'. When she heard her daughter's words, the mother bethought herself, 'This is a trick of hers; she wants me to be off. Why should I go on a pilgrimage? What shall I see if I go? Where my children and my house are, *my* Pandharpur is there.' Tukā says, All such people are entangled in deceitful hopes.

3599

WHAT passes for wisdom with these dolts is sensual pleasure; they give up all their time to lust. If instruction in true knowledge be offered them, they will not forsake bad company for it. Tukā says, We should choose the best company; what else is there to help us?

VIII.—Hypocritical Professions

3600

SHE stuffs herself with rags, and the story goes out that she is pregnant. She counterfeits longings and other signs of the state; but there is no child in her womb or milk in her breast. She is barren after all, says Tukā; and, besides, she has to put up with people's contempt.

3601

THE stuffed skin of a tiger looks like a tiger, but it has not the tiger's disposition. The jeweller's stone detects mere gilding; when it is rubbed upon it, then its nature shows itself. Monkeys may dance as they are taught to dance; but they cannot go beyond that point and invent anything. Tukā says, If a man stores up what is worthless, he will soon be ridiculed for the rubbish he values.

3602

A GLOW-WORM may puff himself up in the presence of the sun, but the world bears witness to both of them. No one can confer beauty on himself, though he may put on airs and parade his own magnificance. If a man drinks whey and boasts of the strength he derives from it, his want of self-restraint betrays the poor diet he lives upon. Tukā says, Fie on the kindness of the *thaga*; after displaying it, he cuts the traveller's throat at his ease.

3603

MERE professions lead to nothing; what we want is a running spring of truth within. As a last resource, a case is decided by fire; we see who can grasp a hot iron without injury. Tukā says, Swerve not from this rule; call that only genuine which is genuine.

3604

WHY should we live on with the mere name of worshippers? Jewels are finery that is bound to perish. Let us exert ourselves, and gain something real; we can then display it openly, and satisfy our desires. Anything is excellent that can be weighed in the scales of truth; but how long will a gilded article deceive men? Tukā says, Do not ruin me, O God, by fettering me to the past and future.

IX.—Indifference to religion and churlish conduct to the saints

3605

HE never even dreams of providing God with a robe; but he sends his wife a costly *sari*. To support a cow never enters his mind; but he caresses his horse with his own hand. He runs after his horde of dirty children to wash them, but he never says, 'Let me bathe the feet of Brāmhanas'. Spit in his face, says Tukā; he goes down to hell to meet his reward there.

3606

HE hugs his wife, bosom to bosom; but when he meets the saints, he draws back from them. He turns his back on a visitor claiming hospitality, but goes forward eagerly to salute marriage-guests. How often would he dream of saluting a Brāmhana? Yet he is like a child in the hands of a Turkish slave-girl. Tukā says, We must not be angry with him; how can any one change his own nature?

3607

THE mouth polluted by abuse of the saints is nothing but a tanner's water-pot. A man who distinguishes not his own from another's proves his mother a whore. He who pries curiously into the life of the good is a *chāndāḷa*; it is a foul pollution to touch him. Tukā says, Reason has been given us to understand this; of this I make no doubt.

3608

THEY slight the saints, they look on Musalmans as Gods; such men are slaves of the belly, all corrupted, O God, by desire. Tukā says, They know not their duties; they are led into error by self-conceit.

3609

A CUR may bark at the heels of an elephant; but he is soon chastised, and suffers for it. What can a fly like him do to such a creature? Yet he worries him, because it is his nature to do so. A full-fed ram may mock at a lion; but this is merely a challenge to death. Tukā says, Vile men may harass the saints, but they only blacken their own faces.

3610

MEN forget the tales of God's life and actions, but they enjoy jest and story. They laugh over these and clap their hands together, but they are ashamed to beat the holy cymbals.

3611

IF a man does not love the company of the Vaishnāvas, we may be sure he was a *manga* in a former birth. Impure in speech, vile in caste is he; he understands not the rule of good behaviour or religion. A piece of aconite tastes sweet, but it ends by destroying life. Tukā says, If a man's father is not pure, he is far from Govinḍa.

3612

THE wicked man has no pleasure in the worship of Hari; he delights in lecherous songs. He sheds tears over the smallest coin that he presents to a Brāmhana; but for sensual pleasures he is willing to be fleeced. He will not give a beggar a rag a span broad; but he bestows rich shawls on play-actors. Spit on his face, says Tukā; he goes to find out what hell is like!

3613

IF a man chews betel-leaves as he sits at a preaching, he will incur the sin of cow-slaughter. If he smokes tobacco there and puffs out the smoke, his sin will drown his household. If he chatters while the service is going on, he will be born again as a frog. The man who dislikes services will be sorely tormented; Yama will lay his rod on his back; his face will be blackened, says Tukā.

3614

TO give up all respect for the saints is a trick of the wicked; a drunken man raves after this thing or that. *You* do not look like drunken men; why do you say what is not right? When a man is lead astray by crazy arguments, you cannot control him; a mongrel ass, without fail, is an obstinate brute. Tukā says, A man whose father cannot be ascertained—such is the man who sees uncleanness in the saints.

3615

HE can never endure hunger or thirst; he runs to see the feats of mountebanks. When pressed to come and hear tales about God, he says 'I have no one to take care of my house'. If you *compel* him to attend service, he lies down on a cushion and goes to sleep. Spit on his face! says Tukā.

3616

HE has little understanding, yet he is a crest-jewel of self-conceit. 'Who is wiser than I'? says he. He shows no respect to any one; he volunteers to persecute the saints. One who censures the saints and harps on their faults, he is soiled by every sin himself. Tukā says, A fraudulent rogue is he.

3617

HE pours forth treasure in offerings to princes; but he will not give away a copper on a holy occasion. He entertains lavishly relatives who come to visit him; but he pounds the husk of grain for the saints. He feeds his wife's relatives willingly; but he drives out his father and mother. It weighs on his mind when he has to invite Brāṃhanas to a *shraddh*; but, afterwards, he sets to work cleaning cow-houses. He will carry water and flowers to a whore; but he will not offer a Brāṃhana a betel-nut. He will work hard at cleaning drains; but he feels too tired to worship God. He is always busy at his trade; he never grows tired of that; but he groans with fatigue when he goes to visit the saints. He goes to sleep when he hears Hari preached; but, at other times, he sits up late for nothing. He never has leisure to listen to the *purāna*; but he plays at dice, day and night. He never casts a glance at the manifestations of God; but he turns his greedy eyes at the places where women bathe. He abhors the water in which Brāmhanas have washed their feet; but he drinks deep draughts of lust. Such men, says Tukā, are entangled in the world from the hour of their birth, they have lost Viṭṭhobā.

3618

IF you set a *vrindāvana* plant in a sugar-cane plot, it will not forsake its bitter nature. If you nurture with fond affection the young of a crow, it will not leave filth alone. If you embrace a wasp's nest, it will set you howling and shouting. Tukā says, There is no good in men like these creatures; they are for ever attacking the saints.

X.—Confidence in learning or merit

3619

IF knowledge of Bramha can so easily be attained, then how is it the Vedas have proved so feeble? Arguments about the Scriptures, the repetition of names, pilgrimages, wanderings over the face of the earth—for this one end were all devised. For this one end did Vyāsa write all his works. To gain this one end, adore the feet of the saints, then, only, you will cross the stream, says Tukā.

3620

IS it a small burden a horse carries? Such is memory—work without faith. Hold fast, says Tukā, to a faith that never wavers, if you seek the Lord of Pāndhari.

3621

TO whom now shall I direct my words? Who will take them to heart intelligently? Do not thou repulse or evade me; this will bring me to utter misery. From house to house people go on talking about knowledge; this will never bring them to the truth. Tukā says, While we are imploring thee for mercy, there comes along some wise fellow and finds fault with us!

3622

I HAVE lost all hope; my mind is now quite tremulous; let Nārāyana soothe it. In patient resolve thou art unwearied; thou art the life of the world; cursed be a life busied with various doctrines. The soul takes fright at the sight of these problems; the toil it has spent on them is all lost. Tukā says, I cannot live without a word from thee; we must watch over the gift you have given us; it is high time.

3623

LET no pedants come within sight of you; these tormenting rogues are void of devotion. Curses on their learning and pride; curses on the face of the wicked! Tukā says, They come to persecute us with their importunities; we shall show them no respect; we shall shave their heads!

3624

LIKE the whiteness of a white leper, is self-conceited pride in knowledge. Who likes it in the bottom of his heart? It is a loathsome sight

By a misprint in the Indu Prakash edition, the last three lines of this *abhanga* are printed as 4376.

when we approach it. No less repulsive is a corpse adorned for burial. Like a meal of filth, says Tukā, are the tricks of those that remain conscious of their bodies.

3625

IN the end, he is left neither this nor that; all his talk is wasted. He is without reward himself; let his cries benefit those who come after him. He finds no dwelling in the sea of bliss, he is full of the conceit of learning. Count him an ass, says Tukā, and thrash him wherever you meet him.

3626

YOU have made yourself a learned man, and you read the *purāna*; but you do not know who you are. Like an ass carrying a load, you turn over the leaves of manuscripts; but, good sir, you do not know the secret of the true teacher. Tukā, the peasant's son, knows nothing about the scriptures; one thing alone he does not forget—the feet of Viṭṭhobā.

3627

IF you count up the interest on a loan advanced in a dream, it will not fill your purse when you awake. Even so, men whose knowledge is all words go on babbling; they make their living by selling knowledge—which no one should sell.

XI.—Various

3628

HE is like a fly that leaves fragrant sandal and sits delighted near a foul smell.

3629

BAGS of sugar are set on the ox; but, after all, he gets dry stalks to eat. Camels carry boxes of precious goods; but they get only thorns. Thus all our efforts are futile; they only multiply our desires, and they hand us over bound to Yama. The man who really gains something, enjoys it; others, poor creatures, exhaust themselves in vain. Learn wisdom, O fool, says Tukā; do not go whirling round in the wheel of the eighty-four.

3630

HE who, for gain, perverts morality or law, his forefathers become worms in hell. He incurs the guilt of murdering a million cows. He makes his father drink the uncleanness of a woman. Yama will sorely torment him, says Tukā.

3631

THE son has turned out a thief; his parents rejoice. Now why should they toil to earn anything? He is smelting gold and making ingots of gold. He brings home his unearned gains, and enriches the house. Both of them feel at ease—

because they are on the way to hell! He is born of a shameless pair; the fruit and seed are both accursed.

3632

AFTER he has heard all this scorn poured on him, should he show his face again, spit on him when you see him. He is a mere dog to live so dishonoured a life. Tukā says, His nature is such that the very sight of him is an evil omen.

3633

IF you find there is no salt in your pottage, the best plan is to be silent. It is not worth while talking to a silly slut of a woman.

3634

AFTER due consideration, we should never fail to punish the guilty. We should tolerate no frivolous arguments; we should not melt lead along with gold. Rules of justice were framed to punish offences; the mere authority of the judge is nothing. Therefore, O God, says Tukā, show me whose the fault is.

3635

SINCE you have the power of speech intact, why do you not shout aloud his name? You are ashamed to cry 'Hari'! You swell with pride as you walk along. You stalk along in the self-conceit of youth like a piebald dog without a tail. In your insensate arrogance, you feel ashamed to dance amid the train of pilgrims. Through the influence of your own jewels, you pass by the *tulsi* wreath. How delicate you have grown! Your health cannot stand the fast on the eleventh day. You never bathe yourself, or put ashes on your forehead; you look complacently on your own skin, yet there is nothing in flesh to help you. Here is Tukā, beseeching with tears him of the Lotus-Navel, the Lord of the World.

3636

SHE starts a conversation with him, though she avoids his open glance; she clings to him for a moment, and then runs after her pots and trinkets. She hides her love under this behaviour; but her own passion ruins her. She inflames him with desire; she wrings his hand, and runs away. She speaks imploring to him, that henceforth she may ensnare him; but her mouth is filled with dirt. How will he ever come back to her? Tukā says, Her own desire brings her to tears. Why do not men serve thee faithfully? Why do they not offer their pleasures to you?

3637

A MAN may please his fancy by eating flesh, but he makes an enemy by doing so. Who would take pity on such a man, seeing that his own life does not teach him what another's life is? He sharpens a knife against the animals who stand before him, but he takes the greatest care of his own little finger. Tukā says, These people pound up bones, and then shed tears over the misfortunes they bring on themselves.

3638

THE poor man says of the fortunate, 'When will he be stripped of his wealth'? He longs to see the other like himself; how can he change his own nature? The dull members of a meeting long to see the learned overthrown. The coward when he sees a hero murmurs feebly against him. Envy not other men; seek the protection of God. Tukā says, How often must I bring shame on the wicked?

3639

THUS, on one impulse or another, do these wretches weary themselves in vain. Why do they not secure their true interests, each so far as concerns himself? Why do they waste their words, with a purpose in view that leads to nothing? Tukā says, Offer something at least to God, and thus serve him.

3640

WHEREVER I look, I see men pounding chaff; I see them licking canes that have been squeezed dry, and expecting to taste sugar. They are deluded souls, O God! I pity them deeply. They are like pressed men carrying rich burdens; their pompous appearance is deceptive; when they reach the halting-place, they must beg an alms. Tukā says, Why this needless mystery? Show your words in close connexion with yourself.

3641

'IT'S this way', 'It's that way' so they cry; but both sides are crazy and senseless. Their conceit pulls them this way, and pushes them that way; but, between the two, they come to grief. There is no room left in them for patience or peace of mind; in the end, they feel the pinch of circumstances. Tukā looks on with amusement while people are boiling with excitement.

3642

CAN prating produce endless bliss? You do but hurt your own vital organs. One man suffers from hemorrhoids; another, with the itch, laughs at him. One man longing for wealth wearies himself with toil; another, who is indolent, laughs at him. A consumptive man says to some victim of disease, 'Stand further off'. A man with sore eyes tells another that his ears are crooked. Tukā says, I bow myself at the feet of all, and beg them each to heal himself.

3643

HATRED of living creatures is a mark of the wicked; they are hard, and lovers of debate. Their inner qualities come to the surface; thus they make themselves known. The good recognize time and season; their heart is pure in all its four corners. Tukā says, I must observe at all times what is prescribed or not prescribed for me to seek.

3644

BY the help of a rope, a man scales a mountain; but he destroys himself over the last footstep. A doctor cures a patient of a hundred and eight disease; the patient kills him to escape paying his fee. A mother bears a child's weight nine months in the womb; he strips her naked, and leaves her in a public place. A man milks a cow, and then ties her up and beats her, and leaves her hungry. Tukā says, A man who reviles God's worshippers —if you look upon his face, it will cast your ancestors into hell.

3645

THESE are all tricks to evade the truth, but the Kali age is round us on every side. It will not be well with us in the end; we ought to feel some fear within us. He will twist your ears; the master is fully awake. Say then, blessed is the Lord, now, while there is time; do not shake your head while you are here. Do not imagine that Tukā will be silent.

3646

YE shaven-headed queans, why do ye keep a store of *kuku*? Spend your time in honest labour for a livelihood; why do ye put on alluring airs? To whom do you show off these graces? You harass your souls for no substantial gain. Tukā says, You self-willed creatures, why this idle vanity?

3647

If we lay a block of wood across a channel, it will hold back a stream of water. Association with a few rogues will ruin a crowd of men. One fly will spoil a lot of food, if it falls into it. Tukā says, Why did his mother give birth to such a fool as this ?

3648

He speaks politely to the prosperous; he spends his own money in making a show before them. Such is the vile character of degraded men; they do not know what they ought to do. They will not pour water on the hands of the thirsty; but they give others sugar even before they ask for it. They go to meet the prosperous and invite them to their houses; but they hide away their bread at the sight of others. They will not speak a straight-forward word to these; to the others, they call themselves sons of their maid-servants. Tukā says, They are mere asses; they waste their lives.

3649

Thus did a wife speak out her secret wishes to her spouse :—' There is no woman so tormented as I am. I am always attending to your concerns, yet every one despises me. You gather round yourself devouring thieves and spies, while all my children are abused. Your mother burns with hatred against me; I cannot bear her eternal scolding. Your sister is always mischievous and spiteful; how can I have any pleasure in life? Your brother is not straightforward, and never speaks openly to me; whose authority am I to recognize? As long as I am with you, you enjoy some peace; but when I am gone, things won't look promising. I do violence to my feelings, and stalk about waiting on you; but you don't feel ashamed yet! Leave your family, and I will manage your concerns; if you don't, I'll kill myself!' Tukā says, Her spouse was the slave of his lusts, and he acted as she desired.

3650

THAT slave of lust thus addressed his wife:—'Why are you always so distressed? My parents, brother and sister, they annoy you; I will leave them. If ever I see their face again, let me be blamed for your death. To-morrow morning I will get up and leave them; I surely will, I swear it. When I have left them, I will make you some bracelets; you are my life's companion. Necklaces and chains,—you shall have them all. I will get you ornaments for your hair; don't be vexed. A fine robe you shall have, with golden spangles, and a flowered bodice.' Tukā says, The vile woman made an ass of him; he ran to meet her wishes.

3651

WHEN the people living in the same town cannot agree with one another, decent people should not stop there. You cannot say what may happen there in a moment. Though you may be innocent, they saddle you with trouble.

They have no love for ancient wisdom; they carry on disputes everywhere. The rogue assaults the honest man, and when it happens, one steps in to prevent it. They hand over the prince's subjects to inconsiderate officials, and get them plundered. It would be better, says Tukā, to find a mountain den, and seek repose therein.

3652

HE scorns instruction; he does not understand his future good. Within this hell of a town, he inflicts sufferings on men; but there are others who have power over him. He stores up vices, and grapples them to his soul. Tukā says, Dullness of comprehension makes men give up purity in deed.

3653

THE sinner who feels no dread will suffer the very perfection of pain. What power will accept and protect him? He shall have no issue; his home shall be deserted; dense darkness shall overtake his family. The man who takes a gift from him, says Tukā, shall suffer the pangs of hell.

3654

HE is wailing now, but when he sinned, he reflected not. He coveted women and wealth; he was a cozener of men. He would betray the credulous, and felt no disgust. Tukā says, He never truly came to life; he was born in vain.

3655

'MY hands are encumbered by shield and sword'; so says some soldier, and asks how he can fight. 'A coat-of-mail, a sword-belt, a horse, and helmet are burdens; they are a second messenger of death. Some one else set me on this horse; how can I run away now?' The weapons of war he calls encumbrances, and cries out, 'What can I do?' Tukā says, He is a very Bramha! Fool! He knows not the secret of the saints' feet.

3656

A CENSORIOUS man is really a benefactor; how can I truly praise his worth? He is something like a washerman—a man of excellent qualities. He washes you gratis, without charging anything, keeps your surface free from defilement. He purifies those who seek to attain, so that they are eminent in the three worlds. His tongue is soap indeed; he cleanses you from the guilt that was born with you. His own destination is the city of Yama; he will dwell in the lowest hell. But I lay myself at his feet, says Tukā; he is a place of purification.

3657

HE is a donkey dressed up like a man; he wags his beard instead of a tail. He lives on scandal; he stores up a heap of sins at home. He sits there, at his ease, and eats them; but, someday, says Tukā, he will go to hell.

3658

THEY manage their affairs with great self-importance; they do not realize that people see their failings. Their sanctity, the members of their own household perceive; out-of-doors, they censure these who have truly renounced the world. They cannot see their own shortcomings; but they enlarge on the demerits of men they meet. Mankind are fast bound by love of sensual pleasures; thus they are entangled in birth and death. Tukā says, My own past has endowed me with a nature that is mad after God.

3659

HIS carnal desire is tortured with thorns; yet he longs to embrace his wife. He is young and good looking; but he has to parade the streets. He is on the verge of manhood, his passions like water gushing from a well-bucket, young and married, yet he has to walk public places. The bride wears a *tulsi* wreath on her neck; the husband pines after her in Vaikuṇṭha. Tukā says, Such is the tale of a husband; he has rejected divine truth, and gained nothing after all.

3660

WHEN a guinea-worm attacks the foot, it is bound up with a piece of cloth, the *bibva*-nut is applied to it—a low remedy for a low disorder. When a servant loses his temper, does the master go to make peace with him? That is another servant's business; the low suits the low. When a maid-servant loses her temper, will her mistress go and pacify her? That is another maid's business; the low suits the low. When a scorpion enters a shrine, we don't think proper to worship him; a slipper is the thing needed, the low suits the low. Tukā says, People of the same class will eat dust for each other's sake.

3661

HIS wife sent out for her mother's house; he gave her his old father for escort. They put some fresh provisions on an ox they took with them. As they went along, the ox threw her down, and the two of them began to abuse each other. She refused to cover herself properly, and there she lay naked. Every one laughed at them; she went on abusing her husband:—'He ought to be ashamed of himself; why are you tormenting me'. Every one spat on them, says Tukā, in their derision.

XX

The Purpose of Incarnations and the use of Images in Worship

3662

FOR the sake of Pundalika he took his stand on the pebbly shore; in endured a sojourn in the womb to support the *rishi* Amba. He is the stay of all the gods; he is the sole author of the holy spells. It is he, says Tukā, whom the Bearer of the Trident contemplates.

3663

WHATEVER we do to him he endures; how trustful he is to us! I have waved my body round him and thrown it away. What! Does he not know how to say Yes or No? or how to wield his authority? Tukā says, He stands patiently, hand on hip.

3664

THIS generous Lord of many kingdoms, the ruler of Vaikuṇṭha, through love for Pundalika stands upon the brick. He, the bestower of all mystic powers, has brought with him all his train; he stills the fears of his worshippers, and says to them, 'This receive'. It is he who created the world, who established the gods and sages, who upheld the twenty-one heavens by his controlling power. Tukā says, Merciful is he, he fulfils our desires; mystic powers, wealth, and liberation, his company will bestow on us at last.

3665

THIS is why the one became two—Nārāyana chose for himself the bliss of devotion. He took to himself a manifest form, his form with four hands; yet he is a seed of one essence, there is no difference of nature within him. He refused to be a mere void, yet he remains without stain; the Absolute stands upon the brick. You may utter his name easily, the utterance delights in it; streams, tanks, and wells hold but one water. Tukā says, This bliss I enjoy; as I utter his name, I feel there is no distinction between us.

3666

BY my faithful devotion I have brought you into a form suitable for me.

3667

IN thy love thou hast assumed a manifest form; this is why thou hast created the wide-extended world. Accordingly, I rejoice to sing thy name; I will not forget it for one moment. This is the secret to master, the essence of all religious duty; all modes of worship are embraced in this. From various points of view, various faiths arise; there is little reason to follow any of them. Tukā says, We shall cast him into the womb of desire, and grapple him to our soul as though he were a little unborn child.

3668

I AM a slave of those who are free from desire, who feel neither pleasure nor pain. He stands on the Bhima's bank, hand on hip; what wonder is it that he comes when you call him? Why, he runs to help his worshippers even when they forget him.

3669

FROM ancient days, thou hast neglected no servant of thine; thou hast accepted those who sought thy protection. About thy feet are set, as badges of thy glory, tales of the protection thou hast afforded to thy worshippers. Tukā says, It was for us thou hadst to make thyself manifest, O Pānduranga.

3670

TO save and protect faith thou dost manifest thyself; thou art a shield to thy worshippers. For the sake of Ambarishi thou didst endure birth; how many of the wicked thou didst destroy for him! Blessed are they who call thee Sea of Mercy! Now make thine own words true. Tukā says, The Purānas declare that Nārāyana is a sea of mercy.

3671

GOD dwells in a visible form at Pāndhari; other images, in all quarters of the world, are but images. You may go into the waste and preach, regarding all stones therein as Viṭṭhala. Tukā says, The chief thing needed is faith; God comes quickly and stands where he finds faith.

3672

IF my words be intended to fathom your nature, let me lose my eyes, O God! Pralhāda did not himself set you within the pillar; you manifested yourself of your own good will. You assumed a form to serve your worshippers; you yourself have neither form, nor attributes, nor name. Is there any one so base that he is not fully assured of your nature? Tukā says, I speak through the fond admiration I feel for you; be not angry with me, O God.

3673

FEEBLE is my intelligence; my ignorant desire, O Nārāyaṇa, is to see you manifest yourself. In all the created world—in stone, and wood, and living things—you show yourself; yet my ignorant desire is to see you, to embrace you with my narrow mind. But you, O chief of Gods, are merciful; your assurances are manifest to the world; you are eager to serve your worshippers, says Tukā.

XXI

False Religious Observances

3674

WHY dost thou shut thine eyes and murmur the names of God, when in thy heart is neither love nor devotion? The name of Rāma is a spell open to all, that banishes the pangs of sojourn in the womb. If you practice the spells of magic with mystic diagrams and charms, you will fall into the world of demons; there is one spell alone that Tukā practices, one name alone that he repeats,— the name of Rāma, the saviour of the world.

3675

THE shrine is vile, the ashes are vile; they have conducted a vile intrigue; the god is vile, the worshipper is vile; he ruins the souls of others. Tukā says, This class of people are all vile together; those who have had experience of them will know what marks them out.

3676

HE wears the ochre robe, but he is a dog by nature; what path of spiritual experience has he followed? He lets his hair grow long, and wanders in every direction; but he has merely reduced himself to the plight of a fox. Some of them dig holes in the earth to live in; but are there not rats enough about? Tukā says, What need is there to act like this? It is idle to torture our bodies.

3677

SIVA, Sakti, Surya and Ganapat—they say these are all one with Vishṇu. They think a flint and a diamond are the same thing; they waste their lives in impure worship. Such as say other gods are God, their life is impure and fit for the impure. It is a foolish fancy they indulge, to bestow Godhead on other gods. My master reveals this by his own mouth; it is no utterance of mine. Blessed are the Vaishnāvas who worship Keshāva; pure are their souls and fit for liberation. Tukā says, Who is there that has not liberation in his power? Submit yourselves to Govinḍa alone.

XXII

Our Attitude towards Traditional Forms of Worship

3678

WHEN a man goes to perform a *kirtana*, he should not partake of food. He should not put fragrant powder on his forehead, or a garland on his neck. He should not demand grain or grass for his horse or bullock. Tukā says, Those who take or give money at such a time go to hell.

3679

WE cannot reach the goal by virtues merely talked about; O God, there is nothing to be gained by these. In you, what makes us marvel is this, that there is nothing you cannot really do if you take it up. I concur not in doctrines concerning the action of our past; in the Purānas we find much that is shocking. Tukā says, At thy feet I have opened up my faith; let it find such accomplishment as thou shalt bring to pass.

3680

IT is not fit that speech of mine should pollute you, O learned Brāmhanas! So I humbly entreat you, give me the leavings of your food. Practise you your duties as they are prescribed in the Vedas. It is your duty to give and mine to receive the food you leave, says Tukā.

3681

GIVE me what I ask for,—an attentive hearing; keep the feet of Viṭṭhobā in your minds. This will appease my spirit; I need no luxuries, no delicacies, no gold. Observe the fast on the eleventh day, keep the pediment for the *tulsi* at your doors, wear on your neck the *tulsi* wreath. The food that such a man leaves uneaten, to me, says Tukā, is a Dasarā, a Divāli.

3682

WHAT are the practices and penances that *we* go in for? What could our fathers have known about them? We chaunt our songs in the assembly of the saints, we stand at their nightly vigils. It is not after our ideas to go and practise renunciation. Tukā says, We shall bring our senses under this delicious mood.

3683

A BRĀMHANA by caste who performs not his ablutions, he is but a Brāmhana in name. He is lower than the lowest if he neglects the *shaligrāma* and keeps company with whores. He will not accept as holy the water in which the saints' feet have been washed; he lusts after women. Tukā says, Do not even look a second time on his face.

3684

THIS practice of penance and contemplation does not attain its end with length of time; but even slow-witted men pass into a trance as they hear thy story. There is nothing to be compared with it in the three worlds, however much we search. Tukā says, To banish my sorrows I continue among the saints.

3685

HE doesn't bite you or hurt you, or shy; he is clean in his habits, he will not eat filth. Still an ass in an unholy creature; you cannot make a gift of him on an holy day. She bites, and kicks, and shies; she yields little milk; her mouth is never clean, and she eats filth; yet a cow is holy and proper for a gift on a holy day. A Brāmhana ought to a Brāmhana for his teacher, and never a Shudra; good customs proceed from God, says Tukā.

3686

WORDS apart from God are a fruitless end to follow; they are like wrestlers employed to amuse a gathering. The performance of prescribed duties, apart from God, is like the pliant smoothness of a reptile's skin. Tukā says, If you are wanting in devotion, you are truly unfortunate.

3687

IF a man sacrifices his life in a sally of desperation, God has no pity on him ; he is like one who throws himself into the Ganges in a fit of annoyance. He attains neither heaven nor liberation, but he does not miss the pit of hell. Tukā says, Remember Kṛishṇa and Rāma and your cares will be dispelled.

XXIII

Against false teachers and impostors

3688

WHAT is the use of these hired monkeys that dance before the world? When Yama searches them, they show their teeth; his satellites drag them over hot iron-rods. They shake their hands and teeth, they play their tricks to win applause. Tukā says, I cannot count how many such bearers of burdens have suffered shame.

3689

THOSE that comfort their bellies by selling the Gayatri, their end is hell; it is the end of such as sell their daughters, or take money for singing God's name.

3690

HE pretends to be busy reciting the names of God, but he lets sleep come over him, till he is quite oblivious to his body; such worship is repulsive; it is like the mimicry of a strolling actor. In his greed for gain, he has sold the service of God; where is God left in such a one? Tukā says, The man who loves honour, we will cover him with shame.

3691

WHAT means this hanging about, like a dog at a palace-gate? Your pretence of freedom from desire is all a hollow mockery. Why have you gathered round you this disorderly crowd of followers? Tukā says, The filth you discharge is something different from your pretences.

3692

WHAT avails it to string together verses after another man's style? What avails it to pound chaff? What is gained by crowding out truth? If you pour out verses, the world will fall at your feet; but he who gives them all this pleasure goes to hell. Tukā says, Unless a man has God on his side, his false pretences will bring shame on him.

3693

THE back is bowed down by this load of their knowledge; their idle chatter never comes to an end. How long must I listen to it? The very scavengers are killed by the stink of drains. Their talk is vapid, unseasoned with salt, dry husks and chaff. Tukā says, These dull fools cannot see their own true interest.

3694

THE worship of God is ruined by a crowd of paid expositors; the rogues love a pompous fraud. They will not eat a meal ready before them; they spoil milk by over-churning it when whey is formed. Even when they are dining by themselves, they must needs have a table; they are so fastidious, they do not know how to take food. Tukā says, The end of it will be their veneer of devotion will actually bring them to hell.

3695

THE preacher expounds at length the knowledge of Bramha; he does not practise it himself. Tukā says, He composes long poems; but he courts honour, as though it were the great thing.

3696

HE puts no faith in God; he derides the saints; he learns the letters of the text by rote; he goes about distressing men with arguments. He declares the gods are stones; he is void of faith, says Tukā.

3697

HE shakes his bag of beads and wags his chin; every bead he tells, he finds fault with some one. His fruit, when it ripens, will be the chastisement of Yama; he has made his home in the furnace of hell fire. He harbours rage in his heart, like a Mang; he barks like a dog, and pretends he is reciting God's names. Tukā says, He has bathed himself in urine, and given his forefathers filth to eat.

3698

IT were better, in one sense, to be a deaf man; but those are mere brutes crammed with learning. All their good-luck has been burned up; why does a luckless wretch go on living? It were better, in one sense, to be crazy; cursed be the argumentative rogue! Tukā says, Creatures that live on a dunghill cannot tell what nectar is.

3699

BE ye as ye may be; we surely shall not distinguish between you; we follow God with single purpose, groping on our way, hand in hand. Why should we concern our minds with your faults or merits? Tukā. says, Why should I suffer anything foreign to affect my mind?

3700

A BARREN woman may feign pregnancy by winding rags round her womb; so two pedants go on chattering, and sell their feigned knowledge to make a livelihood. Mere talk of curry and rice—who would eat it and satisfy his appetite? We may write 'sugar' on a piece of paper; but it will not taste sweet if you lick it? Tukā says, Fie on men's pretentions! They have neither shame nor recollection in their minds.

3701

A PREACHER who has no knowledge of Bramha—of just practices or thoughts—he carries on a traffic in false goods. He was conceived in the womb of a buffalo; he should be called an ass, a *Chandāla.* A man who makes money by preaching—What! Could not the wretch get enough to eat otherwise? He talks nonsense to fill his stomach; but he is never ready with an instructive tale. He is a rogue among mankind, says Tukā; Why did his mother give birth to him.

3702

SOME become religious mendicants and put on saffron robes, and yet forsake not their desire for pleasure. They scorn coarse food, and crave for divine grains; they expect honour and polite attention. Tukā says, Their worship is an arrogant fraud.

3703

SOME let their hair grow long and wear their loin-cloth tucked up; they smear themselves with ashes all over.

3704

SOME pierce their ears and hang large ear-rings in them; they call themselves lords of the world. They go their rounds and demand money, but they never remember Sankara.

3705

SOME dash their heads against the ground; they set themselves bleeding; these are Malanga. They wear goat-skins and iron chains; they shout aloud with might and main.

3706

SOME shave every hair from their heads, and chins, and faces; they wear good garments dyed black. They carry in their hands sticks reversed, and preach their doctrines to all men. They seduce women, and dress them like themselves.

3707

SOME turn themselves into Jangamas, and plaster ashes on their bodies; they blow their shells from door to door. They honour not the flowers and water of their God Śiva; they ring their bells to make a livelihood.

3708

SOME wear marks on their foreheads, and tie wreaths round their necks, and wander from country to country to fill their stomachs. They wrap a white rag round their loins, and search for dainty meals in holy places. Tukā says, They are thugs who deceive men.

3709

IN apparel of these various kinds they roam about ; they beg for alms to fill their bellies. Which of them has renounced the world to seek the Highest ? Tell me truly, prithee, the name of such a one. Shuka abandoned the world in the hour of his birth ; he led a life without stain, says Tukā.

3710

THEY say, We are saved; they are greatly conceited, they are quite deranged and crazy. The rogues waste their lives in quarrels; they seek, by their disputations, to win ease and honour. They go on urging their assertions without any proof of evidence. Tukā says, How many such have gone down to the lowest hell !

3711

WHEN you meet with preachers such as these, you and they will both go to hell. Their preaching of God is more to a man than his own mother; yet they are not ashamed to let it out for hire. They that take and they that receive a price for it are both denizens of hell ; yea, they dwell in the lowest hell. Tukā says, Their greed drags them down to the pit.

3712

HE bears no outward sign of the spirit of the saints; he is not fit for instruction. If a man cannot swim, yet allows another to grasp his waist in water, what can one say to such a fool? If a man who is worn out seeks help from another who is worn out, they will both be brought to the same plight. O Helper of the Poor, says Tukā, let me look on no such man!

3713

If you coat a stone with sugar and set it upright, the crowd will think it genuine. So long as men are mad after sensuous pleasures, some one will deceive the crowd by coating things on the surface. How can such hypocrites serve Hari? They know not what is purity of faith. Tukā says, How can any one be a ṣaint so long as his mind is polluted by lust and anger?

3714

THEY employ agents and go betweens, and force their instructions on men. 'Saints' there are of this kind, who seek a living; how can God be present with them? They get women and children into their clutches, and obtain annuities for themselves. They expound the Scriptures, but they never act according to their own expositions. They act like rogues, says Tukā.

3715

SOME men assume the character of saints to impose on the world, but they are always slaves to their families. A parrot talks like a man, and amuses people; a bull led by a Timmaya behaves as he is taught; a doll will squeak as it is made to squeak. Fie on such skill! says Tukā.

3716

THEY feign to be possessed by spirits, and bestow boons; devotees like this bring mischief with them. They sit in shrines and wave fans; these sinful creatures besmear themselves with sin. Their words are verified by chance like predictions in 'odd and even' games; thus they delude men. If they can control divine powers, how is it their own children die? Tukā says, He who gives away water and ashes is no true worshipper of Kānhoba.

3717

TO fill his belly, he tells tales about worldly characters; he forgets Hari, who sent him into the world. Though he gets his stomach filled with food, he forgets the Purifier of the Sinful. 'Who am I? Whence did I come?' he forgets all about this. He goes on praising the achievements of men; he is a chatterer, says Tukā.

3718

TAKE back your chattering, and give me back my sickle. Your advice is useless, and my white bullock has gone straying.' Tukā tells such people, that the magic-stone will not touch a potsherd.

3719

THE idle talk of a chatterer has no taste nor flavour; he talks always to himself about himself. Who would wish to be killed by his jarring words? The wise should leave him alone. When your ears take in the braying of an ass, what admiration of it would your voice express? Tukā says, The properties of a man's speech will attach themselves to your own person.

3720

To sell preaching is to commit incest with one's mother; the man who takes hire for such a purpose is polluted. The preaching of Hari's attributes is the mother of Hari's worshippers; the man who would make a living by it is a *Chandāla*. The lowest of castes would never do such a thing.

3721

He instructs his pupils that the worship of their spiritual guide is their chief duty. He gives them an example of ceremonial righteousness; he carries the staff, the pot, the wreath; he remembers the ochre robe; but all to no purpose does he call himself a *sanyasi*. Tukā says, If he cannot get rid of lust, he will not gain his end.

NOTES

Abhanga.	Line.	
2655	6	'This place nor that,' this world or union with God.
2660	2	Read *koradi*.
2661	2	A man's destiny is popularly supposed to be written on his forehead.
2682	3	*Chintana* must refer to the contemplation of worldly interests; this is what has been taken from him.
2691	3	Stake, on which he was to be impaled.
2706		The 'treasure' is the experiences, pleasant and painful, which are allotted to a man in the world. A man is not responsible for them. They are sent by God.
2708		Tukā allegorically describes himself in attendance on God under the image of a dog in attendance on his master's house. The 'buttermilk' is in general the refuse of the house, and it represents the favour which Viṭṭhobā graciously spares for his devotee.
2721	1	*Bhat*, a hereditary bard who sings the praises of a chief.
2722		The doors and the approach to the temple.
2728	4	The second half of this line is obscure,
2729	4	The last half of this line is probably corrupt; no translation can be suggested.
2742	3	I look on the water in my body as mere water, on the gas as mere gas, etc.
2756	3	God, read *nivadi*.

Abbhanga. Line.

2761 4 Literally, 'to skin your knee'.

2763 1 A doubtful rendering. *Taka* is a metal plate with an image of a God stamped on it.

2773 Tukā is not speaking of spiritual estrangement from God, but only of giving up visits to Pandharpur.

2777 Presumably, some parent had come to Tukā and complained that he had misled his son.

2780 Apparently directed against a crowd of rich, but insincere, worshippers of Hari.

2782 1 The *Manga* is rage.

2783 It is a fact that Tukā sat in meditation on this hill, but it is not certain that this *abhanga* is by him.

2784 A rather clumsy use of philosophical language, which is probably not Tukā's.

2785 Supposed to be the last words of Tukā.

2793 1 *Bhava*, (i) Faith, (ii) an agreement as to wages.

2801 2 *Vivasi*, a mischievous female spirit, vaguely supposed to be the authoress of human mishaps.

5 We, i.e. Tukā and his brother.

2803 2 Read *Sahya*.

2815 5 The letter prefixed is *Bh*.

9 Read *manase*.

2819 1 These are the two months in which religious assemblies are held at Pandharpur.

2821 3 It is an old superstition that children born feet foremost can see hidden treasures.

2822 3 The three qualities are, *Satva*, *Raja Tamasa*.

Abhanga. Line.

The four animal kingdoms are—
(i) Born from a placenta.
(ii) Born from eggs.
(iii) Born from sweat, e.g. lice.
(iv) Born from seeds (plants).

2826 1 The mention of the *linga* is unparalleled in Tukā, and suggests that this *abhanga* is spurious.

2834 Alandi is a village about fifteen miles from Poona, where there is a famous shrine of Dnyānadeva. As Tukā never writes in honour of this saint, the *abhanga* is evidently a forgery.

2843 3 Read *prakāsha sakalā*.

2844 1 Read *sevene*.

2865 Obviously, all the actions mentioned are impossible, and the poem is a satirical attack on the advaitist view, that we and our actions are unreal and *yet* can be offered to Brahmā.

2866 2 Literally, 'In the place of three and a half cubits.' As this is the traditional measure of a man, the phrase seems to mean vaguely overhead'; and perhaps the translation in the text shows what it meant.

2870 4 *Unmani* is the state of absolute union in which personality disappears.

2871 3 Or else read, 'Has grown upon me more and more.

2879 1 Both strings, i.e. the string that connects men with Govinḍa, and that which connects them with the world.

2880 'This' and 'that' the worshipper and God, or the baby and its mother.

2888 A certain Bhil hid himself in a tree to shoot deer, he broke off some of the branches to

Abhanga. Line.

enable himself to look out, and these he threw down on the ground. It happened that there was a *pinda* under the tree; and Śiva, regarding this as an act of devotion, took the Bhil to Kailasa. So, too, the vulture entered a temple to eat the remains of food offered to Śiva, and unintentionally fanned the *pinda* with his wings.

2900 4 Ajamēla.

2905 10 One of the four commanders of Rāma was a bear, Jambuvanta

2906 A book of omens *(Sortes Virgilianœ)* is used by opening a page at random and reading the passage found. 'What you desire' is a prognostication, not the object desired; thus Viṭṭhala surpasses the book, for he either gives or refuses this object itself. Again, the power of Viṭṭhala to help the sinful is contrasted with the misery they must endure so long as they depend on merit for salvation.

2912 3 The 'platter' is a leaf-dish, which is simply thrown away when done with.

2914 3 This is the only place, so far as I remember, where the title 'Jagannath' is given to Viṭṭhobā. The worship of Jagannath, in Orissa, has many striking affinities with that of Viṭṭhobā, as well as points of difference.

2919 The image of Viṭṭhobā once accepted and drank a cup of milk offered to it by Nāmdēva.

Narsi Mēhta was a saint of Surat who addressed a bill-of-exchange to the Lord of Dvārkā, by whom it was paid.

Dhanji Jat spent all his seed-corn on a feast in honour of the saints, and his fields were sown by Pānduranga.

Abhanga. Line.

Mirabai was a Hindu girl who refused to enter the harem of the King of Bijapur. Her father compelled her to drink a cup of poison, but she was saved by Pānduranga drinking it.

Dāmajipant of Mangalvēdha allowed some famine-stricken wretches to steal grain from the stores of the King of Bedar. Viṭṭhala disguised himself as a *mahāra* and went to the King's court and paid for the grain.

Nāmdēva once, by mistake, began preaching at the rear of the temple of Avindha Nagnath in Berar. The mistake was pointed out by somebody; but Nāmdēva replied that the God in the temple might turn the temple round if he chose. This the God accordingly did.

2920 Episodes in a forest fire, where Govinda saved the lives of certain young creatures.

2928 1 This is a paradox for 'worship' *(puja)* especially.

2934 3 Read *kari te*.

2938 3 A very speculative rendering.

2947 3 The string of the puppets.

2955 1 Literally: 'is carried on the head of.'

2963 Obscure; but seems to mean that as long as we seek *material* blessings, it is no use asking them from God.

2970 2 Read *navha te* separately. Note the occasional sense of *karana* as ceremony.

2985 The pots on the Persian wheel represent each a life in the migration of souls.

2986 1 The life of service is said to be wasted, inasmuch as it does not lead to the absolute union, which, as some critics might say, is the proper object of religious devotion.

Abhanga. Line.

2994 1 A Sanskrit word for 'the fall of a palm-fruit following the perching of a crow on the branches of the tree.' A simile for a pure accident.

3000 3 This line has completely beaten us; we can make nothing of it.

3011 3 *Padara*, the very outside strip of a garment; hence, the lost vestige of anything.

3016 4 Read *Anubhāvā*

3017 3 Properly, a *pradakshana* is a circuit round a temple in honour of the God Tukā says that, in his confusion, he makes a circuit round himself

3054 4 Read *thāva*.

3068 This is apparently satirical; the last line means, 'Raise your hand, if you will, to drive me away like a dog, I will tell the world this is how you treat your worshippers.'

3076 3 Literally: 'You make your waist run away from us'; the waist being the part by which a man would naturally be caught.

3078 If a man clings to the world, the world will cling to him.

A recluse, who declines all intercourse with men, allows his hair to fall in disorder over his forehead.

3100 4 Equal in the service shown and the love given.

3101 5 It seems impossible to find any connection of thought in the last two lines.

3106 Not only the elephant (Gajendra), but also the alligator who attacked him, were saved by Vishṇu. (The belief is that all creatures attacked and destroyed by Vishnu are afterwards saved by him)

Abhanga. Line.

The deer failed to find her fawn; she turned her face up to the sky as an appeal to Vishṇu, who saved her.

3107 4 After this, in other editions, follows 'Nowhere in the three worlds are you to be found acting according to your title.'

3109 1 *Naratsya* should be *narantsya*; it is then an emphatic reduplication of *narendra*.

3112 4 Sc: Will *you* change your word?

3122 2 'The two songs' seems to refer to the two expressions 'our mouths should be saints, our senses ascetics.'

3134 4 The chakra or discus is the weapon of Vishṇu. It is an ancient weapon of Indian warfare.

3148 3 Intellectuality, wealth, courtesy, authority, creative power, strength.

3152 3 *Vāsa* for *vāta*.

3161 4 Hell.

3176 2 Read *mula*.

3186 3 Read *khare*

3190 5 Either a life that respects the good in this world or a life of self-respect, or a life respected by others on good grounds. One really cannot say which.

3193 4 The three letters are the three consonants in the name Viṭṭhala.

3209 4 The usual order is *Godāvari*.

3232 The point is that God has no *earthly* blessings to bestow.

3236 3 *Dai* and *tai* (*Dāva* and *tava*) are greater and lesser degrees of heat

Abhanga. Line.

[illegible] 4 Read *Nārāyana*.

3254 2 *Pahe* apparently means 'is seen.

3255 Read *chode aise*.

3258 4 *Dhure*. The meaning of this word is obscure, and it has not been rendered in the translation.

3260 10 *Nangavati* for *nanangavati*.

3272 A debtor sits at his creditor's door with his head veiled; the angry creditor is here supposed to snatch his covering off him.

3275 5 My teacher Chaitanya.

3276 2 *ādo pati*, 'like a screen'.

3277 An obscure allegorical representation of the derivation and separation of man from God. The 'mother' is the original *māyā*, the creative energy of God; the 'daughter' is the secondary *māyā*, the world. The allegory is then changed into a pun on 'Shankh,' which means, (i) the shell brought to light at the churning of the ocean, (ii) a fool. Mortal man is at once a fool and a relative of God.

3287 If we praise God's qualities, we are really diminishing his glory by ascribing limitations to one who is beyond limitations.

3300 3 Take *jaijane* together as a noun.

3306 2 The cowherds are a type of the unlearned.

3320 1 Lakshmī is the goddess of wealth.

3326 The Gopī is the soul; the forest, the world; the beasts of prey, temptations.

3328 6 Seems to mean, 'The man who avoids the mistake of cultivating a liking for the remedy, and who does not take it when he is not

Abhanga. Line.

suffering from the complaint, avoids making a vice of it.'

3334 The last line of the Marathi is not pointed in the Indu-Prakash edition.

3343 2 The water supports it.

3345 This may also be translated solely with reference to God and his worshippers.

3347 'So much gained,' i. e. having had a human body bestowed on us.

3351 The *hansa* is a sort of goose; but we do not regard this bird with the admiring eyes of Hindus, so perhaps the word is best left untranslated.

3355 Rāma owned all this wealth (captured from Rāvaṇa); yet, when he died, none of his wealth followed him to heaven.

3361 2 Read *olāvā* for *bolāvā*.

3370 2 One of the classes lower than Shudras.

3376 3 So the Marathi seems to mean, and the meaning suits the context; but this is not the usual view of the operation of the magic stone.

3385 2 They are not absorbed in God, as the Advait school recommend, but keep their own individuality.

3389 3 Read *vitale*.

3435 3 Read *vise*.

3438 Possibly, 'Learn to find things sweet, though there is no actual sugar in them; when you can accept the conditions of life in this way, you are near God.'

3440 2 Read *chintu* in one word.

3443 3 Read *vimukhta*.

Abhanga. Line.

3450 Read *āsakara* as one word.

3468 3 Sarcastic.

3478 The jackal who closes his mouth over an egg is a symbol of the worshipper who has attained union and is silent. The donkeys are the argumentative pundits

3504 Read *uchambale*.

3509 5 In the hour of death you will not be able to utter God's name.

3540 2 Literally 'God suffers'; practically a careless expression for 'matter of luck.' That line means that careless people cut their days short and say, 'It is all a matter of luck.'

3546 21 Vimvasi. See 3008.

26 *Avindha*, 'unbored', is a term for a Musalmān, because his ears are unbored, i.e. he does not wear ear-rings.

3548 4 *Ashā* (hope), *Māyā* (illusion) are used in a double sense.

3553 2 Literally, 'Did he not take his soul into his head,' this being a physiological explanation of a trance.

3558 3 I.e., It loses its bitterness.

3562 '*Pachava*', the return of a disease nearly cured, in consequence of venturing too early abroad and exposing one's-self to the evil-eye.

3565 The covert point of this *abhanga* is, that if a worldly man endures everything for his worldly purposes, a religious man ought to be willing to endure the same trials in the name of religion.

3568 2 This is supposed to be said by some one lending his pots to a neighbour.

Abhanga. Line.

3586 A pun on *shanka*, which means (i) a fool, (ii) a shell. The shell was one of the sacred objects (mentioned in the *abhanga*), obtained at the churning of the sea. The whole is a pointless affair, translated solely on the ground of its obscurity.

3587 The point is that some people are naturally incapable of understanding spiritual truth.

3595 The *murali* is a girl married to a deity, who, having no means of livelihood, supports herself by prostitution. Many girls in the Deccan are still in this position.

3602 4 More familiar to English readers as 'thug'.

3602 3 Obscure. The point seems to be that whey, though nourishing, is a cheap kind of diet; and the man in the illustration, by disclosing the fact that he lives on it, draws attention to his own poverty.

3607 A chāndāla.

3617 10 'The manifestations of God' are the saints.

3620 4 The demon supposed the tortoise to be a rock, as he could not see his hands and feet; accordingly, he stood on him and the tortoise took him by surprise.

3621 2 In modern Marathi, perhaps *dainyakalā*.

3622 2 For *atra tatra*.

3626 3 Tukā was born of a *kunabi* (peasant) family which had adopted the calling of a *vani* (grocer).

3629 5 The eighty-four rebirths.

3636 The behaviour of a man to the world is compared to that of a woman who feels an illicit passion for a man, which she is afraid altogether to avow or indulge. This only ends in her disappointment and misery.

Abhanga. Line.

[illegible] 1 Possibly because the animal he ate may eat him in the next incarnation.

[illegible] 3 *Gosawali* is a Persian word meaning a dealer in the chief commodity; here used as an equivalent for yama.

[illegible] Seems to picture the position of a husband with a vicious wife, who drives him out of doors. Thus, in spite of himself, he leads a life of enforced chastity, which, after all, brings him no nearer holiness.

'In Vaikuntha,' perhaps 'even after he is dead.' *Ridē*, the leather bucket which brings water out of a well.

[illegible] 1 Perhaps *pasāra* should be taken, more correctly, solely of the shrine of Pāndhari and its surroundings.

[illegible] 4 Read *mita* for *nita*.

3674 3 Or, 'you may learn to control the demons.'

[illegible] This *abhanga* is directed against those who will not be satisfied with devotion, when it is a course easily open to them, but persist in carrying on theological discussions till the spirit of religion disappears. They are compared to a man who ever churns milk, etc.

[illegible] 3 The Mangs are a low caste, formerly employed as executioners, etc.

[illegible] 2 'Divine grains,' rice and wheat. This *abhanga* describes the *Sanyasi*.

3703 This described the *Birāgi*.

3704 This describes the *Kanphatya*

[illegible] The *Malanga*.

3706 The *Mānbhāva*.

3707 The *Jangama*.

Abhanga. Line.

3715 3 Some beggars lead about a sacred bull, which is taught a few tricks and earns a few coppers.

3718 Some rustic is reviling a preacher and regretting the time he has stopped his work to listen to him.

Various phrases, etc., used by Tukā.

The Baudhya Incarnation. This refers to Buddha. The popular view recognizes so much of the Buddhist system as to understand that the Buddha retired to *Nirvāna* and gives no direct answers to men. Consequently it looks on him a sort of heartless God, more or less appropriate to the Kali age.

The Kali Age. The word has no connection either with Kalī (the consort of Shiva) or with *Kala*, Time. It means 'confusion', and is applied to the present age of the world's history, from which all distinctions and sense of propriety in conduct have vanished.

INDEX

Showing the correspondence between the numbers in this edition and those in the Indu-Prakash edition of 1869. English No. 2649 in the translation is No. 3177 in the Indu-Prakash edition. The Marathi No. 2649 will be found in the index to the preceding volume to be No. 2116 in the English translation.

CPSIA information can be obtained
at www.ICGtesting.com
Printed in the USA
LVOW04s1309130716
496166LV00026B/440/P